THE FOOD AND COOKING OF
ARGENTINA

THE FOOD AND COOKING OF
ARGENTINA

65 TRADITIONAL RECIPES FROM THE HEART OF SOUTH AMERICA

CESAR BARTOLINI

Photography by Jon Whitaker

aqua marine

This edition is published by Aquamarine
an imprint of Anness Publishing Ltd
108 Great Russell Street, London WC1B 3NA;
info@anness.com
www.aquamarinebooks.com; www.annesspublishing.com

If you like the images in this book and would
like to investigate using them for publishing,
promotions or advertising, please visit our website
www.practicalpictures.com for more information.

Publisher: Joanna Lorenz
Executive Editor: Joanne Rippin
Additional text: Wendy Hobson
Photographer: Jon Whitaker
Food stylist: Jayne Cross
Props stylist: Joanna Harris
Designer: Adelle Mahoney
Production Controller: Wendy Lawson

© Anness Publishing Ltd 2014

A CIP catalogue record for this book is available from
the British Library.

PUBLISHER'S NOTE
Although the advice and information in this book are
believed to be accurate and true at the time of going to
press, neither the authors nor the publisher can accept
any legal responsibility or liability for any errors or
omissions that may have been made nor for any
inaccuracies nor for any loss, harm or injury that comes
about from following instructions or advice in this book.

NOTES
Bracketed terms are intended for American readers.

For all recipes, quantities are given in both metric and
imperial measures and, where appropriate, in standard
cups and spoons.
Follow one set of measures, but not a mixture, because
they are not interchangeable.

Standard spoon and cup measures are level.
1 tsp = 5ml, 1 tbsp = 15ml, 1 cup = 250ml/8fl oz.

Australian standard tablespoons are 20ml. Australian
readers should use 3 tsp in place of 1 tbsp for
measuring small quantities.

American pints are 16fl oz/2 cups. American readers
should use 20fl oz/2.5 cups in place of 1 pint when
measuring liquids.

Electric oven temperatures in this book are for
conventional ovens. When using a fan oven, the
temperature will probably need to be reduced by about
10–20°C/20–40°F. Since ovens vary, you should check
with your manufacturer's instruction book for guidance.

The nutritional analysis given for each recipe is
calculated per portion (i.e. serving or item), unless
otherwise stated. If the recipe gives a range, such as
Serves 4–6, then the nutritional analysis will be for the
smaller portion size, i.e. 6 servings. The analysis does not
include optional ingredients, such as salt added to taste.

Medium (US large) eggs are used unless
otherwise stated.

Contents

Introduction

Ever since I can remember, food in my family has been served freshly prepared with the best ingredients available. We never had frozen chicken nuggets; we would have home-cooked escalopes coated in fine breadcrumbs. Food prepared from scratch has always been central to my family life, as it is in the lives of most Argentinians.

Above: One of the carefully kept vineyards in the region of Mendoza, which produces Argentina's famous Malbec wine.

Fresh and simple

Like many in Argentina, my grandfather was an Italian immigrant who moved to Argentina after the Second World War with my grandmother and one of my aunts. They settled down and raised a family, so my mother and her sister were both born in the country. Grandad ran a greengrocer's shop for many years and also grew vegetables and fruits in his garden, so we were never short of fresh produce. The back yard also housed his chickens and rabbits.

We spent much of our time with my grandparents, and it was a great treat for me to pick fruit straight from the trees, help my grandmother pick lettuce, tomatoes, beans and herbs, and collect eggs for the family meal.

If there was anything we couldn't collect from that productive garden, we could find it just walking distance away at the local butchers, bakers and fishmongers. A trip to the big supermarket only happened once a month to stock up on storecupboard essentials. At the weekend we would go to the market where the variety of produce was even more extensive.

For anyone interested in food, that might sound idyllic, and it certainly was for me. Nor was it unusual, or a thing of the past. This is the way most Argentinians still source their food: fresh, local and home-grown. Pre-prepared ready-meals are rarely seen or eaten as there is no need for them. Even if there is no time to cook, you can easily grab great, freshly cooked food from the local shops or market stalls.

A family of cooks

My grandmother and grandfather, mother, aunt and uncle are all very good cooks. My grandmother was also a great baker and we

Left: The little town of Iruya, Salta province in northwestern Argentina, clings to the mountainside. It was first settled by Amerindians whose earliest roots go back to the Ocloyas, a people from Kollasuyo, which became one of the four regions of the Inca empire.

Above: Alfajores, cookies sandwiched together with dulce de leche, are a favourite mid-morning snack for children.

Top middle: Empanadas and beer, a favourite after-work snack for office workers.

Top right: Churros in a bakery in El Chalten, a village in Santa Cruz province.

Below: The traditional drink of Argentina, yerba mate, is served in a cup with a metal straw.

particularly loved her homemade sweets and cakes. My uncle also used to give cooking lessons to his mates as a hobby. As soon as I was old enough I began to help out in the kitchen. By the time I was about 15, I knew that all I wanted to do was to be a chef and by the time I was 18, I had not only completed my secondary school education, I had also graduated with a diploma in culinary arts.

My love affair with food – and particularly Argentinian food – has continued. I love the flavours, the succulent meats, the colourful, crisp vegetables, and I embrace the passion with which the Argentine people approach their food – as they approach life – and bring it into the heart of their day.

Eating through the day

Some say that breakfast, desayuno, is the most important meal of the day; certainly no one ever missed it in our house. Toast with homemade jam or our favourite caramel sauce, dulce de leche; pastries, homemade cakes or cereals, with tea, coffee or yerba mate for the adults, were our staple fare.

Mid-morning snacks are often alfajores, our national cookies. At the weekend when we visited the market, we might be treated to freshly cooked churros, long, sugar-dipped fried fritters. A light lunch – almuerzo – might be a slice of pizza, or perhaps a steak with salad and fries. This, of course, is for the urban dwellers. In the countryside, something more substantial is

required, and a hot meal of grilled beef, corn and potatoes would be carried to the workers so they could enjoy a well-earned rest during the hottest time of the day. Lunch is also time for empanadas, delicious little pastries with various fillings.

The late afternoon sun brings out a British tradition, when many Argentinians enjoy a cup of tea with a sandwich or a slice of cake. Later, colleagues and friends congregate in cafés, or confiterías, to drink espresso or cold beer and share picadas: small dishes of bread, cheeses, mussels, salami and cured meats, anchovies or fish pâtés, very similar to Spanish tapas.

Dinner, cena, is the largest meal of the day and eaten late. Drinks or cocktails are served around 8pm, followed by a meal that may not begin until 10pm, and is likely to carry on for a couple of hours. A great social occasion, we would often gather for cena at my grandma's house, and certainly on special occasions, when my godfather, a keen fisherman, might bring a freshly caught dorado for the table.

Sunday is when we eat the asado, the ultimate barbecue and the heart of Argentinian cuisine. Even for an everyday family barbecue, size matters, and the asado has to have a table groaning with grilled meat and sausages.

This wonderfully generous and hearty spirit of hospitality is probably what best typifies the food and cooking of Argentina, a spirit of happy abundance that the recipes in this book will help you to recreate and enjoy.

The land and its riches

The passionate national pride Argentinians have for their country definitely influences the way they feel about their food and cooking, so the history and geography of the country, its climate and the regional specialities are an essential part of understanding Argentinian cuisine.

Soaring to the rugged, majestic mountain ranges of the Andes at the summit of Cerro Aconcagua, and plunging to Salinas Chicas on the coast, South America's second largest country can boast variety of all kinds: from glaciers to deserts, from rich agricultural plains to snow-capped mountains, from indigenous peoples maintaining their old lifestyle to the sophisticated and cosmopolitan café culture of the capital, Buenos Aires.

Running down the spine of the continent, the Andes forms Argentina's western border, but the majority of the country is lowland, and vast tracts of land are fertile and productive, making it one of world's greatest food-producing nations. With its extensive Atlantic coast, along which the warm Brazil current alternates with the cold South Atlantic waters, Argentina enjoys an abundance of seafood in its coastal waters, which is exported around the world.

The Pampas and the gauchos

Vast grassland areas in the centre of the country make up the Pampas, the Guarani Indian word for 'flat plain'. These fertile lowlands with deep, rich soil, gentle temperatures and generous rainfall are ideally suited to agriculture. In its northern area, the lands were often planted with wheat, although over-cultivation has now become a serious problem. These days the most common arable crop is soya beans, but it is for its cattle that the Pampas is justly famous, home of the beef industry in a country where beef is king.

Cattle was introduced to the Pampas from Paraguay in 1580 and now the region is home to 4 per cent of the world's cattle – around 54 million head – spread across vast ranches

established in the 19th century. Many ranches have been converted to guesthouses, where tourists can enjoy the beautiful countryside, but others remain active farms, raising vast herds.

These animals are still tended by the gauchos. Synonymous with the Pampas for at least two centuries, the gauchos have, in fact, been herding cattle – and hunting deer – since the original wild cattle roamed the plains. Their nomadic life suggests that the name gaucho is from the Mapuche Indian term 'cauchu', meaning vagabond. And most gauchos have some indigenous Indian blood.

Accomplished horsemen, strong, proud and independent, many have now adopted a modern style of dress, but some still cling to the old traditions, with their facón knife tucked into a sash around their bombachas, the comfortably loose trousers, and a poncho thrown over their shoulder. They are renowned for their horseriding prowess and their skill with the tirador or

Above: The incredible autumn colours of the lower slopes of the Andes mountains.

Below: The leaves of the yerba plant, grown extensively in Mesopotamia, are picked, dried and infused to make the national drink, yerba mate.

Right: The traditional facón knife of the gaucho, tucked into a highly decorated belt.

Far right: Gauchos herd sheep near Lake Argentino on the grasslands of Patagonia.

slingshot, bolas – three leather-bound rocks tied with long leather straps – and their leather whips. They display these skills at local rodeos, where succulent steaks are cooked on huge grills and served to the enthusiastic audiences.

Mesopotamia

In the land between two rivers – the Paranà and Uruguary – water is the dominant influence in the warm, fertile wetlands and rain forests. Here, fruit is the primary crop, and oranges, tangerines, grapefruit, mangoes and papaya all find their way to the markets. This is also the home of the yerba plant, an evergreen shrub related to holly. The leaves are infused to make yerba mate, enjoyed everywhere, from the campfires of the Pampas to urban cafés.

Gran Chaco and north-west Argentina

The dry region in the far north of the country, densely forested in the east and sloping to broad grasslands, also records some of Argentina's highest temperatures so tends not to have a strong agricultural focus. The salt flats on the Chilean border are surrounded by

peaks of up to 4,000 metres (13,125 feet), while further east the rivers carve the land into deep canyons. Winters are dry and warm, while heavy rains fall in the hot summers, making this the perfect location for the sugarcane industry.

Cuyo

Home to the 'roof of the Americas', Cerro Aconcagua, and also acres of lush vineyards that make this the centre of the wine-making industry, where the Malbec grape has become synonymous with Argentinian wine.

Patagonia

The rolling high plateau of Patagonia, with its cold, often snowy, winters and temperate summers was supposed to resemble the hills of Wales, although the Welsh settlers who arrived there found it more rugged and certainly more windswept. On these ranches, sheep rather than cattle are the animal of choice, and while the finest Argentinian beef comes from further north, Patagonia supplies wonderful lamb, and barbecues here favour the local meat, while fruits and vegetables include root crops that flourish in temperate regions.

Buenos Aires

Ideally situated on the busy waterway of Rio de la Plata, the outlet of the Paraná and Uruguay rivers, the capital and most prominent city of Buenos Aires enjoys an enviable climate: changeable in spring, hot and humid in summer, with a mild autumn and winter, and a moderate rainfall throughout the year. Over 20 per cent of the world's honey is produced here. and vineyards produce fine-quality wines.

Below: The General Belgrano Bridge spans the Paraná River and connects the northern cities of Corrientes and Resistencia.

Argentina's culinary heritage

This beautiful landscape provides the backdrop to the lives of an exuberant and passionate people. Although evidence of habitation has been found dating back 13,000 years, Argentina was sparsely populated by the indigenous peoples, who lived as hunter-gatherers on the broad plains. Today, pockets of the Onas, Yamanas, Tehuelches and Mapuche tribes all preserve that traditional way of life, but the predominant cultural and culinary influence in the country is Spanish.

Argentina's population was transformed by the arrival of Europeans, and the culinary legacy of the indigenous people now remains only as a backdrop. However, although 90 per cent of Argentinians are of European extraction, 56 per cent of those have at least one Amerindian ancestor. The highest numbers of immigrants in the 19th century came from Spain and Italy, with the result that anyone familiar with Spanish and Italian cookery will feel at home in an Argentine kitchen, where they might also recognize some subtler influences from Britain, France, Russia and Eastern Europe.

The conquering Spanish

It was in the first years of the 16th century that the glistening river, Rio de la Plata, and the view of snow-capped mountains inspired the name Argentina – from the Latin *argentum*, silver – and not, as might be expected, mineral riches. But while Argentina is the only South American country where the gold-hungry Spanish and Portuguese failed to find their precious metals, it is a country rich in many other ways.

Early settlements were intermittently established on the site of modern Buenos Aires, and began to flourish as new immigrants arrived in the country. Throughout the next century the region was part of Viceroyalty of Peru, controlled from Lima, but by the end of the 18th century, the Viceroyalty of the Rio de la Plata was established in Buenos Aires, annexing not only modern Argentina but also parts of Uruguay, Paraguay and much of Bolivia. Trade in this fertile region flourished, with beef and associated products at the heart of this important commercial centre.

World politics intervened, however, and with little official Spanish support, the viceroyalty failed. But Spanish immigration continued, and individual Spaniards continued to settle in Argentina. Between 1880 and 1890, almost

Above left: An old colonial Spanish church, the Iglesia de San Pedro, in the small town of Fiambalá in the western part of the Province of Catamarca.

Above: The beautiful, brightly coloured woven fabrics of the indigenous tribes of Argentina are sold in village markets throughout the country.

Right: A typical grocery store in Buenos Aires clearly shows a Mediterranean influence in the ingredients used by Argentinians on a day to day basis.

Far right: A group of women in Patagonia celebrate their Welsh ancestry, by gathering for tea, cakes and scones.

Below: A mounted gaucho herds cattle in the evening sun at Estancia San Isidro del Llano, Buenos Aires Province.

one million immigrants arrived from Europe, most of them coming from Spain and Italy.

This influx of people has provided the bedrock of Argentine cooking with ingredients such as bell peppers, tomatoes, lemons, olive oil, garlic and Mediterranean herbs flavouring the beef, lamb or seafood. Don't be surprised to find pizzas and pasta dishes on the menu with Milanese-style escalopes and empanadas.

More contributions to the melting pot

Political unrest and wars brought many more immigrants to Argentina. At the turn of the 19th century, France, Spain and Britain were all involved in conflict that impacted on their colonies. This led to more settlers coming from England and France and, as Spain's power appeared to weaken, to the beginnings of a fight for Argentine independence, which was

declared in 1816. Bringing investment, crops and expertise into the new country helped development and modernization, and the continuing European influx strengthened the economy and stamped a European style on the people, the agriculture and the food.

Among other British immigrants at the end of the 19th century, Patagonia saw an influx of Welsh people, who established vibrant communities on the windswept hillsides, and dotted them with sheep, windmills, chapels and Welsh names. Visit the region and you will be sure to be offered lamb, Welsh cakes and even leeks. Enclaves of Irish immigrants also chose to settle in Patagonia, where one of the staple crops is potatoes. The 19th century also witnessed German immigrants establishing communities in the west of this region, bringing their dark rye breads and apple pastries.

Around the same time, the French began moving into Argentina, many from the Basque region. Prior to that, most French emigrants had opted to go to Uruguay, but the changing political climate there meant they were no longer so well received. Assimilated into the local population in Argentina, they nonetheless congregated naturally in regions where vines would flourish, and many of the people who live in the Mendoza region are of French extraction. Along with wine, French-style pastries find their way on to many Argentine breakfast tables.

Other cooking styles have been absorbed into Argentinian cuisine with traditions from the immigrant peoples of Eastern Europe, especially the Baltic states, Lebanon, and many Jewish communities.

Argentine beef and the asado

No country for vegetarians, beef is at the heart of the cuisine in Argentina, where they eat more meat per head than any other nation. Certainly no celebration in Argentina would be complete without the asado – a barbecue on a grand scale that clearly demonstrates the generosity of spirit, strong sense of family, and simple joie de vivre of the Argentine people.

Argentine beef

The beef is of supreme quality, and Argentina's national dish comes from the Pampas, where the gauchos roasted the meat on a spit over an open fire, then shared the tender meat, cutting off chunks with their knives. Because they are grass-fed rather than corn-fed, the beef has a wonderful flavour and succulent, tender texture. Add to that a high degree of culinary skill and you get perfect results, to such an extent that waiters will cut the steak with a spoon to show diners how tender it is.

The scope of beef dishes in homes and restaurants is extensive, from simple grilled steaks to rich casseroles, such as the slow-cooked beef stew, puchero. Stews and casseroles – carbonadas – are often teamed with local sweet potatoes and corn, which is grilled in its husk on the barbecue or parilla. Boned joints are also served, rolled around a tasty stuffing. Another universally favourite dish, which is especially enjoyed by children, is deep-fried milanesa de ternera, thin slices of beef coated in breadcrumbs, like an Italian or French escalope. Milanesas are made not just with beef but also with chicken or veal.

Another popular meat dish is escabeche, a traditional method of preserving meat or fish by marinating it in lemon juice or vinegar either after, or instead of, cooking.

The asado

While for Argentinians it may be commonplace, to a visitor the asado is, quite simply, amazing, and represents the most influential culinary tradition in the country.

While there is no need for a proper parilla, many Argentines have a huge open grill in their garden, although they are more than happy to improvise with a pile of bricks and a steel rack if necessary. Every festival day and many Sundays, they fire up the parilla, laying out the meat in impressive quantities, together with blood sausage, bread and spicy sauces – such as the favourite chimichurri sauce, a hot and spicy mixture of dried red chilli peppers, paprika, lemon, oil and parsley.

The cook, or asador, is most definitely in charge of the proceedings – and it is usually

Above: Beef skirt is a very popular cut of meat for the grill in Argentina.

Left: The climax of a barbecue is the spit-roasted whole animal, either pork, lamb or even a whole side of beef, known as the asador. When cooked still in its hide it is called asado con cuero.

Right: Two of Argentina's favourite offal dishes: calf's liver in higado con cebollas, top, and tripe stew, or locro, bottom.

Above: The person in charge of grilling the meat is also known as the asador, responsible for making sure each course is ready in the correct order.

Below right: A garden in Barreal in the Calingasta Valley with the built-in oven – horno de barro – made with clay, and perfect for slow cooking.

the male of the household. To help him in his task, an assistant keeps watch over the progress of the meat, learning the tricks that will eventually make him a good asador: remembering to season the meat generously before you start to cook; putting the meat over the heat when it is searingly hot, so the meat is instantly sealed; and leaving the pieces well alone while they cook to perfection.

Assistants will learn how to cook steaks, ribs, and strips of sirloin, and create delicious mixed grills – parillada – of lamb chops, jointed chicken pieces and whole fish. And they will have to become adept at slicing and grilling the traditional black pudding, morcilla, that is always part of the asado.

Asado is offered to diners in three courses. Firstly, they are served the black pudding, chorizo and provoleta from the grill, with chunks of bread and chimichurri sauce. Provoleta is made by sprinkling a thick slice of the local Provolone cheese with oregano and chilli, and wrapping it in foil.

The second course is offal, including sweetbreads and kidneys, and also the skirt and flank meat. Finally, the main meat is cut into pieces or sliced, and served to the guests.

Some cooks may also use a horno de barro, an outdoor wood-fired clay oven, or wrap parcels of food and push them under the hot

embers, a technique known as rescoldo, or slow-cook some dishes in a cast-iron caldero suspended over the coals. The pièce de resistance of the asado is also called the asador: originally an Arab method of fixing a butterflied whole beef, lamb or pig to a cast-iron cross, then cooking it beside the flames.

Offal dishes

In Argentina, nothing is wasted, so while in some countries, achuras, or offal, has a limited appeal, in Argentina it is embraced with enthusiasm. Calf's liver is often fried quickly with bacon and onions; in higado con cebollas, it is served still pink in the middle so that it is tender and juicy. Kidneys are served lightly sautéed, often infused with garlic as in riñones al ajillo, or in a tomato and olive sauce provençal. Beef or lamb sweetbreads, considered a delicacy, are softly bathed in white wine to create mollejas al vino blanco. Ox tongue is a slow-cooked favourite, served with a vinaigrette to make lengua a la vinagreta. Cow brain is served in a garlic and parsley sauce.

One of the national dishes of Argentina is locro, a rich, slow-cooked stew originating from the Andean villages and made with tripe. Buseca is a combination of tripe with tomatoes, peppers, beans, red wine and pungent herbs, traditionally enjoyed with a glass of red wine, and callos a la Madrileña combines tripe with pork. Beef heart is very slowly cooked with onions in mollejas de corazón al verdeo.

Argentina's ingredients

Spanish influence is the most easily identified element of Argentine food, with a wide range of Hispanic ingredients, favourite dishes and styles of cooking, which hark back to colonial times. Italian flavours, however, like garlic, onions and tomatoes and Mediterranean herbs, and other European influences are also evident. Few traditions from indigenous peoples are still found in Argentinian cuisine, other than corn and potatoes, and these are mainly cooked European fashion.

Meat and poultry

Argentina's livestock farming offers the broadest scope and quality, so as well as beef and offal, there are many choices on the menu.

Patagonia is the source of the finest lamb, replacing beef in the asado and served with sausages, potatoes, homemade bread and red wine. Small cuts, such as lamb chops, are also grilled on the parilla, and boned lamb joints are stuffed with herbs such as rosemary, roasted then sliced, as in pechito de cordero relleno. Goat is also very popular in Patagonia.

The most common pork dish is fresh chorizo sausages, part of the asado, but also served in a rich and tasty stew, chorizo a la pomarola, that owes much to the rural tradition of hearty lunches for farmers in the fields.

Bondiola and choripán are types of fresh pork sausages, made from neck meat spiced with salt, pepper, paprika and nutmeg. I love choripán served in a sandwich, and bondiola a la riojana, in a garlic and tomato sauce. Tenderloin is another popular choice, sometimes tenderized in dark beer, while in regions where there has been immigrants from Eastern Europe, you will find delicious suckling pig.

Not as popular as in Europe, chicken appears on Argentinian tables in thin breadcrumbed milanesas, or sometimes in fresh salads like salpicon de ave. Chicken is also cooked in cheese sauces, such as pollo al Roquefort, or in wine that is spiced with lemon.

Venison and game

Game has always featured on the tables of the indigenous tribes, and it continues to be popular, especially on the vast grasslands of Patagonia. Venison is often served with sharp fruit to offset the richness of the meat, as in lomo de ciervo con cerezas, in which it partners cherries. Wild game birds like partridge also feature on the menus, sometimes cooked en escabeche. Like Peruvian ceviche, the meat is marinated in lemon juice or vinegar.

Rabbit is far more popular than in Europe and is another dish that is slow-cooked, Mediterranean-style, with garlic, mushrooms and wine to make conejo a la cazadora.

Above: Partridge is abundant in the grasslands of Patagonia. Argentina is a popular place for game shoot holidays, and there are many lodges or hunting ranches that host tourists looking for sport.

Below, from left to right: ox tongue, tripe, kidneys and chorizo sausage.

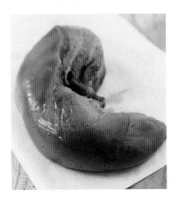   

Right: Empanadas and humitas (corn parcels) being made in a local restaurant.

Below, from top to bottom: Dorado, whitebait, squid, and river trout.

Fish and shellfish

On the coast and in cosmopolitan Buenos Aires, fresh seafood is often on the menu, while inland, you will find more river fish.

Seafood dishes include gambas – prawns (shrimp), and langoustines, along with centolla – king crab – squid, octopus and mussels. Whatever is freshest is combined to make a thick and filling stew called cazuela de mariscos. The larger whole fish may be simply grilled, or fillets breaded and fried to make croquetas de pescado, while smaller fish such as whitebait are fried and served with lemon as cornalitos fritos. In typical Spanish style, cod is often preserved in salt as bacalao and then cooked 'a la vizcaina' with oil, garlic, onions, tomatoes and red peppers. A more unusual dish is caldillo de congrio, a soup made from conger eel. Merluza – hake – is of the finest quality, as is pollack, which often features in a casserole called abadejo al ajo arriero.

Dorado is the primary river fish caught, along with other varieties such as surubí, boga and pacú, primarily in Mesopotamia. Dorado has a rich, oily flesh and golden skin. Sometimes it is encased in salt and baked, the succulent flesh revealed when you break open the salt casing. It is also simply grilled whole and served with potatoes. Salmon and trout are found further south, and baked with Mediterranean herbs or with the contrast of an orange sauce as in trucha con hierbas y naranja. A Peruvian culinary influence is shown in fish marinated 'en escabeche', such as ceviche de salmon con pomelo rosado y palta, salmon marinated in pink grapefruit juice and served with avocado.

Empanadas

The classic pastry snack, empanadas, are found everywhere, in homes and restaurants, and on sale in cafés, bakeries, supermarkets and from street vendors.

Originating in Spain, it is said that the Spanish copied the Moorish samosa, which has been a delicacy of north-western Spain since medieval times. Like a closed pizza or a pasty,

the name actually means 'to wrap something in bread', emphasizing how ideal they are for eating on the go. In most regions, the wrapping is made with a flour and olive oil pastry – as were the original Spanish empanadas – but sometimes puff or filo pastry is used.

Favourite fillings often include cheese – perhaps with ham, onions or vegetables – but minced (ground) beef, chicken, and onion are also popular, usually with a generous layer of cheese on top. There are so-called vegetarian empanada options, but this is not a lifestyle choice readily understood in Argentina, so even if you choose the spinach filling or corn in a white sauce, you may well find it topped with a layer of ham and cheese.

Each region has its own speciality, dividing between those that are baked, Salta-style, and those that are deep-fried, Tucaman-style. In northern Argentina, the smaller salteñas favour spicy beef fillings with potato, egg, red bell pepper and spring onion (scallions). Those from Jujuy, on the Bolivian border, use beef, chicken, goat and llama meat, and spice their fillings with chilli and onion.

Local ingredients are commonly used, so moving into the Pampas, empanadas are almost exclusively beef, while in Patagonia, they may contain lamb, and on the coast they are likely to prefer seafood empanada fillings. A little way south to Catamarca and La Rioja, on the Chilean border, you'll find a different combination of minced (ground) beef with garlic, potatoes, onions and olives.

There are also sweet empanadas, filled with milk-soaked rice and currants or adding sugar and currants to the meat ingredients.

Vegetables, pulses and fruits

Because the country is so extensive and enjoys such a variety of climates, fruit and vegetable available often reflect the locale. Squash features heavily, particularly butternut squash and zapallito, a dense-textured squash with orange flesh. Squash, (bell) peppers and aubergines

(eggplants) are all seared on the asado, or aubergines are baked, Italian-style, with Parmesan cheese, or marinaded in vinegar in berenjenas en escabeche. Pizzas are everywhere, usually topped with tomatoes, (bell) peppers, meats and other Italian ingredients, but also served with an onion topping in fugazza. Palm hearts are very popular, and often served in salads.

Along with potatoes, one of the crops grown by the indigenous peoples, the yellow-fleshed sweet potatoes, batata, remains popular, especially further south and in the mountains. Also in the cooler areas, root crops like turnips find their way into many dishes, especially thick, stews. Argentinian cooks also sauté the young turnip tops before they get too mature and become bitter. Soya beans, butter (lima) beans and chickpeas are made into a flat bread called faina, or are included in hearty soups.

The Mesopotamian region is the centre of fruit cultivation, from where olives, avocados, figs and lemons find their way to Argentine kitchens. Watermelons are a favourite, but other types of melon are also served as a refreshing appetizer or as part of a dessert. Quince and grapes are also widely cultivated.

Cheese

Although some cheeses are imported, the locally made versions are popular, including Manchego, provolone and Roquefort, made from unpasteurized ewe's milk and introduced to Patagonia by the French, while ricotta came with the Italian influence. Provolone holds its shape well so is often grilled as part of the first

Above: From top left to right, sweet potatoes, white corn, courgette flowers and soybeans.

Below left: A sign outside a farm in Salta Province advertises goat's cheese.

Below: Roquefort cheese.
Bottom: Provolone cheese.

Above: Fresh figs, top, and a bowl of dulce de leche.

Below: A bottle of Argentina's popular beer, Quilmes.

Below middle: Glasses of Malbec wine in the vineyards of Mendoza; the snow-topped Andes in the background.

Below right: A gaucho prepares a gourd of yerba mate.

course of the asado. The mild, soft cheese, queso fresco, is combined with quince jelly to make the classic dish of queso et dulce, while a Patagonian speciality, soft goat's cheese, is delicious drizzled with honey.

Sweet things

Argentinian desserts are really sweet and often feature the classic sauce, dulce de leche, a sticky caramel made from boiled milk.

As an afternoon snack or sweet treat, alfajores are light, golden cookies sandwiched together with dulce de leche; some may be chocolate-covered, others rolled in coconut or icing (confectioner's) sugar. Familiar in any Spanish city as the breakfast or mid-morning snack of choice, the long sugar-dipped doughnuts, churros, are usually accompanied by a cup of hot chocolate, made almost entirely melted dark chocolate, as in the best Madrid cafés. Others might prefer buñuelos – deepfried fritters – served with a cup of yerba mate. Medialunas are the Argentinian version of the French croissant and provide a versatile breakfast served with coffee.

Arrope is a by-product of the wine industry, a conserve made from the grape must, which is often used in pastries. Dulce de cayote is a preserve made with a local squash, or the local sweet potatoes, while dulce de higos is made from figs. All these preserves are baked into pastries or tortas fritas, a kind of doughnut.

Rice is popular in Italy so it is not surprising that it features on Argentine tables, cooked with milk and encriched with mascarpone to make a creamy dessert called arroz con leche. Whisking hot sugar syrup into an egg and milk mixture gives ambrosia its wonderfully smooth creamy texture that, with a twist of lemon rind, perfectly complements a shortbread biscuit.

And to drink …

The national drink of yerba mate was originally made with rainwater by gauchos on the Pampas. Made from yerba leaves infused in hot water in a calabash gourd, or mate, the leaves expand to fill the mate and the liquid is sucked out through a silver bombilla, a straw with a strainer to retain the leaves in the gourd.

In the cafés of the major cities, there is a range of local coffees and chocolate drinks available. Alternatively, you might be attracted by a leche merengada, a thick milkshake made with sugar and whisked egg whites.

Although Argentina is renowned for its wine production around Mendoza, drinking and exporting many bottles of Malbec wine, other Argentinian wines are drunk in the country rather than exported, such as vino patero, which is made of grapes pressed barefoot.

Argentina is less well known for its beer, although some excellent brews are made in the country, especially in the south where German communities settled. Quilmes is the most famous brand. Clericot, a fruit cup made with white wine, cider or sparkling wine, makes a delicious aperitif and the indigenous peoples still ferment corn to make a drink called chica.

Celebrating with food

Argentinians express their natural passion through football, dancing and carnivals. As a strongly Catholic country, religious celebrations feature strongly but there are also festivals to celebrate food and wine, folklore, and even gauchos. Whatever the occasion, you can be sure that eating and drinking will play a central role in any Argentinian fiesta, sporting fixture or family celebration.

A good place to start in defining what food means to the Argentinians is to think of its iconic images. These must include gauchos in their distinctive garb, riding their horses across the vast Pampas; the sensuous tango; the café culture of the city; and the harsh environment of the mountains. In addition to these are events, like football matches, street carnivals, and family gatherings for a traditional Argentinian asado. These occasions are always fuelled with food that is of the best quality, cooked simply, with strong flavours and generous helpings.

Café culture

The confiterías of Buenos Aires are important meeting places, and in times of festival are even busier than usual. While most cafés were founded by Spanish immigrants, the majority of restaurants are run by Italians, and the influence is often visible in the menus. Escalopes, ravioli and gnocchi are all to be found.

Street food

On all the street corners, you'll find rotiseria selling local cheeses, cold meats and Malbec wine, delicious sausage sandwiches, and empanadas piled high. If you prefer something sweet, there are ice creams and sorbets, candied apples and alfajores.

A passion for football

Football is a huge part of Argentinian life; it is in their blood and for many people football will take precedence over almost anything else. I've been going to watch Club Atlético Banfield since I was a baby and I love everything about it: watching the game, mixing with the fans, the atmosphere at the ground and the street food. And it's the food that fans enjoy, not drink – no alcohol is allowed in football stadiums. Choripán, sausage sandwiches with chimichurri sauce, is the food of choice for football fans, along with milanesa sandwiches and burgers.

Tango

In August the whole of Buenos Aires gets involved in the tango festival. Featuring dancing in the street, tango shows, classes, and milongas – dances open to everyone – the festival culminates in a national competition.

Carnival

Originally the festival to celebrate the start of Lent, carnival takes place on Shrove Tuesday all over Argentina with lavish parades and late-night partying. Because meat is forbidden in Lent, fish is served with corn and pulses, and finger-shaped shrimp sandwiches – bocaditos – are sold by the street vendors.

Above: The legendary football sausage sandwich, choripán.

Top left: A selection of picadas, little snacks, served in Italian-style cafés in Argentina's cities.

Below: A rural backyard asado for an extended family meal.

Above: While many cities in Argentina celebrate carnival, there is no place that lives and breathes it with the same intense feeling as the Province of Corrientes in the north.

Above right: Loaves of rosca de reyes, the traditional sweet bread, baked during Epiphany.

Below: The annual tango festival in San Telmo, the oldest barrio in Buenos Aires.

Political celebrations

There are many national and local festivities throughout Argentina to commemorate particular historical events. New Year's Eve is also the anniversary of the Constituent Assembly of 1813, and 25 May is the anniversary of the beginning of the 1810 May Revolution, when traditional dishes are locro and tortas fritas.

Christmas and New Year

Festivities begin on 24 December, when families, friends and neighbours gather together, everyone bringing a contribution to a cold buffet, as the weather is really hot around that time. Cured meats and cheeses, stuffed eggs, cold veal with tuna sauce, marinated fish, empanadas, prawn (shrimp) cocktail, nuts, marinated aubergines (eggplants), olives and salads, are spread on the table. That might sound like enough, but the main course is, of course, the asado, served with more salads, perhaps tomato and onion, or fresh mixed leaves. Ice cream, cake or peaches are most usually served for dessert.

As soon as the clock strikes midnight, we pop the champagne or open the cider, light the fireworks and start opening the presents. Once that is over, there is time for more refreshments: pan dulce – Christmas cake – and pastries, whole nuts, chocolates, nougat, turrones, and dried figs and other fruits. That will give us the energy to party until around 3am. Most people forego breakfast for a long lie in, and gather for a late lunch around 1pm.

When New Year comes around, we enjoy another big reunion with a similar spread, but this time the asado centrepiece is pork cooked a la cruz, the whole carcass opened flat into a cross shape and slow-cooked over the barbecue coals. It is said that the reason we choose pork for our New Year feast is to bring good luck at the start of the year as the pig is the only animal that doesn't walk backwards.

A favourite drink is clericot, a cocktail of red or white wine, sugar, lemon juice and sparkling water. Originally invented by British expats in the Punjab, it was adopted by the Argentines who modified its name, claret cup, to clericot.

Epiphany

The festival of the kings, celebrated 12 days after Christmas on 6 January, is a special day for children. They leave their shoes by the bedroom window, to hold presents from the three kings, with grass and water for the camels. Children also enjoy rosca de reyes, a sweet yeast cake topped with icing, glacé cherries and sugar, and shaped in a ring to symbolize the kings' crowns, and God's unending love.

Easter

At Easter, the Argentines do not eat red meat or drink wine for a week, so meals revolve around fish. Children decorate hard-boiled eggs and receive gifts of chocolate. Torta de pascuas, a crown-shaped caked topped with crème pâtissière and cherries, would never be missing from our table at Easter.

Soups, Sides and Salsas

Traditional soups are based on vegetables and are hearty and sustaining. Side dishes and salsas are usually something to accompany the much more important meat.

Crisp, fresh vegetables and tangy side dishes

Meat may be the most important element in an Argentinian meal, but when vegetables do make an appearance they are usually bursting with flavour and very fresh. Salads and sides are often served as part of a cold buffet before the main dish – often an array of grilled meats, and frequently including fish or shellfish. Lettuce, peppers, tomatoes and onions are favourite ingredients, as are root vegetables and squash.

Soups are almost a meal in themselves and often contain beans; they are not usually puréed but are left as a clear broth with chunky vegetables.

Various salsas are served with grilled meats and fish to add a burst of colour and flavour. Chimichurri is probably the most popular, and is almost always available at home and in restaurants. It is a lovely tangy green sauce, full of lemon juice, herbs and chilli, although the Argentinian version isn't as hot and spicy as some South American recipes – Argentinians prefer flavour to heat!

Right middle: A gaucho rides a deserted sun-dappled road in Patagonia, while storm clouds gather in the mountains.

Butter bean soup

Sopa de porotos

This wholesome soup, typical of the thick, hearty soups of Argentina, is popular during the cold winter months. It is easy to prepare, although you need to soak the dried beans ahead of time. Canned beans may be used to make a quicker version.

1 Drain the beans and put them in a large pan and cover with cold water. Bring to the boil, cook for 10 minutes, then lower the heat. Simmer for 15 minutes until the beans are starting to soften. Drain and set aside.

2 Rinse out the pan, then add the butter and heat until melted. Add the chopped onion and cook gently, stirring, for 5 minutes, or until the onion is softened and translucent, don't let the onions brown. Add the garlic and cook gently for a further 2 minutes.

3 Add the carrots, leek, celery and turnip to the pan, and cook for 3–4 more minutes, stirring frequently. Return the beans to the pan.

4 Pour the stock into the pan, bring to a boil, then lower the heat to a gentle simmer and cover with a lid. Cook for 20 minutes. Add the butternut squash and potatoes, re-cover the pan and cook for a further 15 minutes or until both the beans and vegetables are tender.

5 Season the soup to taste, then ladle into warmed bowls and sprinkle with chopped parsley. Serve with thickly sliced country-style or French bread.

Cook's Tip Two 400g/14oz cans of butter beans, drained and rinsed may be used instead of the dried beans. Add them in step 3 for the last 10 minutes of cooking time.

Serves 6

200g/7oz/generous 1 cup dried butter (lima) beans, soaked overnight, or for at least 6 hours

50g/2oz/¼ cup butter

1 onion, chopped

2 garlic cloves, finely chopped

2 carrots, diced

1 leek, chopped

1 stick celery, thinly sliced

1 turnip, diced

2 litres/3½ pints/8 cups vegetable stock

½ butternut squash, diced

2 medium potatoes, diced

salt and ground black pepper

30–45ml/2–3 tbsp chopped fresh parsley, to garnish

country-style or French bread, to serve

Energy 242kcal/1017kJ; Protein 9g; Carbohydrate 35g, of which sugars 8g; Fat 8g, of which saturates 5g; Cholesterol 18mg; Calcium 76mg; Fibre 10g; Sodium 476mg.

Beef broth with vegetables
Sopa de verduras en caldo

Serves 6

50g/2oz/¼ cup butter

1 onion, chopped

2 garlic cloves, finely chopped

2 carrots, diced

1 leek, thinly sliced

large pinch of saffron threads

150g/5oz/¾ cup long-grain rice

2 litres/3½ pints/8 cups beef stock

½ butternut squash, diced

2 medium potatoes, diced

100g/4oz/1 cup frozen peas, thawed

salt and ground black pepper

freshly grated Parmesan and warm crusty bread, to serve

Good beef stock is an essential base for this soup, which is traditionally made using the beef bones leftover from a lunchtime asado (barbecue), to provide a light evening meal. When home-made stock is not available, use a high-quality chilled commercial stock, rather than a stock cube.

1 Heat the butter in a large pan until melted, add the onion and cook gently for 5 minutes, or until the onion is softened. Add the garlic and cook gently for a further 2 minutes. Add the carrots, leek and saffron and cook for 2–3 minutes, stirring frequently.

2 Sprinkle over the rice and stir for a minute to coat in the juices, then pour in the stock. Bring to the boil, lower the heat and cover the pan with a lid. Simmer for 10 minutes.

3 Add the diced squash and potatoes, then re-cover the pan and simmer for 15 minutes more, or until the vegetables and rice are tender. Stir in the peas and season to taste with salt and pepper.

4 Bring to the boil and cook for a minute, then cover the pan with a lid and leave to stand for a few minutes before serving. Ladle into warmed bowls and sprinkle with grated Parmesan. Serve with warm crusty bread.

Energy 247kcal/1039kJ; Protein 6g; Carbohydrate 40g, of which sugars 6g; Fat 9g, of which saturates 5g; Cholesterol 18mg; Calcium 58mg; Fibre 5g; Sodium 406mg.

Baked aubergines
Berenjenas a la parmegiana

In the late 1800s and early 1900s thousands of Italians emigrated to Argentina, bringing their culinary skills and tastes with them. This popular dish is a typical example of their influence on Argentinian cuisine and is excellent served with grilled or barbecued meat or as a delicious dish in its own right.

1 Trim the aubergines and cut lengthwise into 2cm/³⁄₄in slices. Sprinkle with salt and place in a colander. Leave for at least 30 minutes to allow the bitter juices to be extracted.

2 To make the tomato sauce, heat the oil in a pan. Add the garlic and gently sizzle for 1 minute, then add the tomatoes and sugar.

3 Simmer for 15 minutes until slightly thickened. Reserve a few sprigs of basil for garnishing, then shred the rest and stir into the sauce. Season to taste with salt and pepper.

4 Preheat the oven to 180°C/350°F/Gas 4. Rinse the aubergine slices, drain and pat dry with kitchen paper. Lightly dust the slices with flour, shaking off any excess.

5 Heat a little of the remaining oil in a large frying pan until hot, then fry the aubergines a few at a time until dark golden brown and tender. Add more oil to the pan when necessary. Lift out the slices with a slotted spoon and drain on kitchen paper to remove excess oil.

6 Spoon a thin layer of the tomato sauce into a large, shallow ovenproof dish or roasting pan. Arrange a layer of aubergine slices on top, then spoon over more sauce, mozzarella slices and a sprinkling of Parmesan. Repeat the layers until all the ingredients are used up, finishing with tomato sauce, mozzarella and Parmesan.

7 Bake for 30–40 minutes or until the top is golden brown and bubbling. Garnish with the reserved basil sprigs before serving.

Serves 4

4 large aubergines (eggplants)

about 120ml/4fl oz/¹⁄₂ cup olive oil

plain (all-purpose) flour, for dusting

2 mozzarella balls, approximately 200g/7oz each, sliced

25g/1oz/¹⁄₃ cup grated Parmesan cheese

salt and ground black pepper

For the tomato sauce

30ml/2 tbsp olive oil

2 cloves garlic, finely chopped

2 x 400g/14oz cans chopped tomatoes

pinch of sugar

a small bunch of basil leaves

Energy 699kcal/2897kJ; Protein 26g; Carbohydrate 13g, of which sugars 12g; Fat 61g, of which saturates 21g; Cholesterol 64mg; Calcium 480mg; Fibre 9g; Sodium 526mg.

Marinated aubergines
Berenjenas en escabeche

Serves 4–6

4 medium aubergines (eggplants)

20ml/4 tsp finely ground rock salt

475ml/16fl oz/2 cups white wine vinegar

475ml/16fl oz/2 cups water

1 onion, finely chopped

4 cloves garlic

15ml/1 tbsp dried oregano

5ml/1 tsp dried chilli flakes

2 bay leaves

15ml/1 tbsp black peppercorns

250–475ml/8–16fl oz/1–2 cups extra virgin olive oil

Variation Instead of using the various herbs and spices in this recipe, try substituting 45ml/4 tbsp of chimichurri sauce.

Most households will have a jar of this spicy and succulent pickle in their refrigerator. It's a favourite with both hot and cold roasted meat and is equally good with Argentinian cheeses such as provolone.

1 Rinse the aubergines and pat dry with kitchen paper. Cut into 2.5 x 7.5cm/1 x 3in strips. Sprinkle with salt and put in a colander set over a bowl, then place a plate on top. Place a few weights on the plate and leave for 30 minutes to squeeze out the moisture.

2 Pour the vinegar and water into a large pan and bring to the boil. Remove from the heat.

3 Pat the aubergines slices dry with kitchen paper to remove excess salt, then add to the pan, cover and leave to marinate for 2–3 hours.

4 Drain the aubergines and gently squeeze out as much moisture as possible with your hands..

5 Sprinkle the garlic, oregano and chilli flakes over the pieces, coating as evenly as possible. Pack the aubergines tightly into large sterilized jars, adding the bay leaves and peppercorns.

6 Pour in the olive oil, making sure that the aubergines are completely covered. Cover and seal the jars and store in the refrigerator for at least 3 days before serving. Eat the pickle within 3 months.

Energy 358kcal/1476kJ; Protein 3g; Carbohydrate 7g, of which sugars 6g; Fat 34g, of which saturates 5g; Cholesterol 0mg; Calcium 29mg; Fibre 5g; Sodium 336mg.

Sautéed turnip tops
Grelos salteados

Introduced to Argentina by the Italian community, this is an excellent accompaniment to richer meats such as pork and lamb. Make the most of this vegetable while in season and choose young turnip tops (also known as 'turnip greens') if possible, as they become slightly bitter and tougher when larger.

1 Wash the turnip tops in several changes of cold water to remove any dirt or grit. Drain and shake dry in a colander.

2 Heat the oil in a large pan, add the onion and cook over a low heat for 5 minutes until almost soft. Add the garlic and chilli and cook for a further 2–3 minutes, stirring, to soften.

3 Add the turnip tops to the pan, with just the water clinging to the leaves.

4 Cover the pan with a tight-fitting lid and cook over a low heat for 10 minutes, or until completely wilted and tender. Season to taste and serve straight away.

Serves 4

1kg/2¼lb turnip tops, washed

60ml/4 tbsp olive oil

1 onion, finely chopped

4 garlic cloves, thinly sliced

1 fresh red chilli, seeded and thinly sliced

salt and ground black pepper

Energy 158kcal/650kJ; Protein 1g; Carbohydrate 5g, of which sugars 3g; Fat 15g, of which saturates 2g; Cholesterol 0mg; Calcium 22mg; Fibre 2g; Sodium 5mg.

Chicken salad
Salpicon de ave

This creamy yet light chicken salad is ideal for a light supper or cold buffet dish, especially during warmer summer weather, as all the ingredients can be cooked in advance and the salad assembled at the last minute.

1 Put the chicken in a small pan and pour over just enough stock to cover. Bring to the boil, cover, and simmer gently for 15 minutes or until tender. Leave in the liquid for 5 minutes, then remove and leave to cool. Cut into chunks.

2 Meanwhile, cook the potatoes and carrots in lightly salted boiling water for 6–8 minutes or until tender. Steam the asparagus over the vegetables to cook at the same time. Add the peas to the potatoes and carrots for 2 minutes.

3 Drain the potatoes, carrots and peas and set aside to cool.

4 Plunge the asparagus tips into iced water to stop them over-cooking, then drain and cut into small pieces.

5 Put the mayonnaise in a large bowl and season with salt and pepper to taste. Stir in the chicken and cooked vegetables. Peel the hard-boiled eggs and cut into quarters.

6 Arrange the lettuce leaves in a large shallow bowl or plate and pile the chicken mixture on top. Arrange the egg quarters and olives on top, then sprinkle with chopped parsley. Serve straight away with crusty bread.

Serves 4

1 large chicken breast fillet

chicken stock, for poaching

500g/1¼lb waxy potatoes, peeled and cut into 2cm/ ¾in cubes

2 medium carrots, cut into 1cm/½in cubes

1 bunch asparagus, trimmed

100g/3¾oz fresh peas

60–75ml/4–5 tbsp mayonnaise

2 Little Gem (Bibb) lettuces

2 hard-boiled eggs

12 black olives, pitted

salt and ground black pepper

chopped fresh parsley, to garnish

sliced crusty bread, to serve

Energy 325kcal/1359kJ; Protein 21g; Carbohydrate 25g, of which sugars 4g; Fat 17g, of which saturates 3g; Cholesterol 143mg; Calcium 59mg; Fibre 5g; Sodium 352mg.

Palm heart and prawn salad

Ensalada de palmitos y camarones

Serves 4

2 firm ripe avocados

250g/9oz canned palm
hearts, drained

2 Little Gem (Bibb) lettuces

300g/11oz peeled cooked
prawns (shrimp)

30ml/2 tbsp fresh chives,
chopped, to garnish

For the Marie Rose sauce

1 large lemon

60ml/4 tbsp mayonnaise

15ml/1 tbsp tomato ketchup

5ml/1 tsp Worcestershire
sauce

5ml/1 tsp brandy

dash of Tabasco sauce

salt and ground black pepper

This dish became famous in the mid 1920s at the 'golf club' resort in Mar del Plata. Located on the Atlantic coast in the Province of Buenos Aires, this is one of the country's busiest fishing ports. Each January, it hosts the Festival of the Fisherman when huge quantities of delicious seafood dishes, such as this one, are served.

1 Half the lemon and squeeze the juice from one half. Put 5ml/1 tsp juice in a jug (pitcher), then add the mayonnaise, tomato ketchup, Worcestershire sauce, brandy, Tabasco, salt and pepper. Whisk together with a fork.

2 Peel and slice the avocados. Toss in the rest of the lemon juice, to prevent them browning.

3 Cut the palm hearts into 1cm/³/₄in thick slices. Slice the lettuces into bitesize pieces.

4 Arrange the lettuce on a large plate and top with sliced palm hearts, avocado and prawns. Drizzle the sauce liberally over the salad and then sprinkle with chopped chives. Serve with thin wedges of lemon.

Energy 282kcal/1173kJ; Protein 20g; Carbohydrate 5g, of which sugars 4g; Fat 20g, of which saturates 4g; Cholesterol 213mg; Calcium 110mg; Fibre 1g; Sodium 1419mg.

Steak sauce
Chimichurri

Makes about 300ml/
½ pint/1¼ cups

1 onion, finely chopped

4–5 garlic cloves, finely
chopped

2.5ml/½ tsp dried chilli flakes

5ml/1 tsp dried oregano

5ml/1 tsp paprika

5ml/1 tsp salt

2.5ml/½ tsp ground black
pepper

15ml/1 tbsp lemon juice

75ml/2½fl oz/⅓ cup red
wine vinegar

150ml/¼ pint/⅔ cup extra
virgin olive oil

50g/2oz/1 cup finely chopped
fresh parsley

This Argentinian classic is used as both a marinade and a sauce when having asados, parrilladas or cooking in an open pit (all traditional barbecues). It is a must for serving with grilled steak, and is an essential addition to the sausage sandwich, choripán, but is also delicious with fish, chicken, and vegetables.

1 Mix together the onion, garlic, chilli flakes, oregano, paprika, salt and pepper in a bowl. Add the lemon juice and vinegar, then stir in the oil, a little at a time.

2 Stir the parsley into the sauce, then spoon into sterilized jars. Seal and store in the refrigerator. It will keep for 2–3 weeks, but once opened, it should be used within 3 days.

Energy 1449kcal/5960kJ; Protein 5g; Carbohydrate 16g, of which sugars 10g; Fat 144g, of which saturates 21g; Cholesterol 0mg; Calcium 144mg; Fibre 6g; Sodium 1990mg.

Creole sauce
Salsa criolla

This is a quick, light and refreshing sauce that complements any meat or fish, especially more subtly flavoured ones. Unlike chimichurri, it only keeps for 3–4 days and is best made a couple of hours before serving.

1 Put the onion in a medium bowl with the vinegar and salt. Stir well and leave to stand for at least 15 minutes.

2 Add the garlic, chopped peppers, spring onions and tomato to the bowl and stir well.

3 Stir the olive oil, parsley, pepper and cumin into the pepper and tomato mixture, and check the seasoning. Cover and chill for at least 2 hours before serving to allow the flavours to develop. Serve at room temperature alongside meat or fish dishes.

Makes about 475ml/
16fl oz/2 cups

1 Spanish (Bermuda) onion, chopped

120ml/4fl oz/½ cup white wine vinegar

15–30ml/1–2 tbsp salt

2 garlic cloves, finely chopped

1 red (bell) pepper, finely diced

1 green (bell) pepper, finely diced

2 spring onions (scallions), finely sliced

1 beefsteak tomato, diced

250ml/8fl oz/1 cup olive oil

15ml/1 tbsp finely chopped fresh flat leaf parsley

ground black pepper and cumin

Energy 2468kcal/10168kJ; Protein 8g; Carbohydrate 39g, of which sugars 34g; Fat 252g, of which saturates 36g; Cholesterol 0mg; Calcium 124mg; Fibre 13g; Sodium 5949mg.

Provençal dressing
Salsa provenzal

This is one of the simplest dressings to make, which is probably why it features in countless dishes, including grilled and steamed fish and shellfish, baked tomatoes and pasta. It originated from French settlers from the South of France, but unlike the French version, the Argentinian recipe doesn't include tomatoes.

1 Put the garlic, parsley and white wine vinegar or lemon juice in a bowl and whisk to combine. Add the oil gradually, and keep whisking. Season to taste with salt and black pepper.

2 Use straight away, or store in the refrigerator and whisk or shake just before using. To make this in a jar, simply add all the ingredients and shake vigorously.

Serves 4

4–6 cloves garlic, finely chopped

1 small bunch of flat-leaf parsley, finely chopped

30ml/2 tbsp white wine vinegar or lemon juice

100ml/3½fl oz/scant ½ cup olive oil

salt and ground black pepper

Energy 232kcal/955kJ; Protein 1g; Carbohydrate 1g, of which sugars 0g; Fat 25g, of which saturates 4g; Cholesterol 0mg; Calcium 13mg; Fibre 1g; Sodium 3mg.

Portuguesa Sauce
Salsa Portuguesa

Serves 4

45ml/3 tbsp olive oil

2 Spanish (Bermuda) onions, sliced

2 garlic cloves, sliced

1 red (bell) pepper, sliced

1 green (bell) pepper, sliced

3 beefsteak tomatoes, chopped

few sprigs of fresh thyme

1 bay leaf

15ml/1 tbsp dried oregano

15ml/1 tbsp paprika

salt and ground black pepper

Characterized by colourful, richly-flavoured ingredients, this sauce, which is often used with oven-baked dishes, is typical of the recipes that were brought by the Portuguese who came into Argentina from Brazil.

1 Heat the oil in a pan and add the onions. Cook over a low heat for 2–3 minutes, stirring occasionally until beginning to soften.

2 Add the garlic and peppers and cook for a further 3 minutes, stirring frequently.

3 Add the tomatoes, thyme, bay leaf, oregano and paprika. Season with salt and pepper. Cover with a lid and cook for 2–3 minutes. Uncover and cook for 3–5 minutes more or until the mixture is fairly thick and most of the liquid has evaporated.

Energy 178kcal/742kJ; Protein 3g; Carbohydrate 15g, of which sugars 12g; Fat 12g, of which saturates 2g; Cholesterol 0mg; Calcium 40mg; Fibre 5g; Sodium 20mg.

Tortillas, Croquettes and Pastries

Argentinians love to snack, and bakeries, patisseries and street stalls everywhere will sell delicious, freshly cooked little pastry packages or fried croquettes to be eaten on the move.

Tempting, sustaining and delicious

Finger food or little tapas-style dishes are served in all the bars, cafés and stalls throughout Argentina, and cooked at home for hungry returning school children and workers.

Pizza is very popular, in part due to the country's heavy Italian immigration in the early 20th century. Local versions include the fugazzeta, a pizza made with mozzarella cheese and onions, and the fainá – made with garbanzo bean flour with no topping – generally served as a side dish or a base to regular pizza.

The empanada, sometimes baked, is usually deep-fried and can be filled with beef, fish, ham and cheese, or neapolitan (using the same toppings as that pizza). Sandwiches are usually served hot, like the tostado or the lomito; the latter having a great number of versions, with food stalls offering all kinds of combinations.

At home, traditional snacks like the double-crust zapallito tart, or tamales – savoury parcels wrapped in corn leaves – are cooked in large quantities for extended family get-togethers, and crunchy, fried croquettes are cooked and consumed by the dozen.

Right middle: The vividly coloured landscape of Patagonia, with the Andean mountain range in the background.

Fish croquettes
Croquetas de pescado

Most Argentines follow the traditions of the Catholic church and refrain from eating meat on the days leading up to Easter, beginning with Holy Thursday. Fish dishes, therefore, feature prominently on the menu at this time and these croquettes are a popular choice.

Serves 4

200g/7oz fresh salmon, skinned

100g/4oz white fish, skinned

115g/4oz smoked haddock, skinned

1 garlic clove, peeled and halved

few sprigs fresh thyme

about 475ml/16fl oz/2 cups milk

300g/11oz/4 cups warm mashed potatoes

25g/1oz/2 tbsp butter

50g/2oz/1 cup mixed chopped fresh herbs, such as parsley, chervil, dill, tarragon or chives

30ml/2 tbsp wholegrain mustard

2 egg yolks

115g/4oz smoked salmon, chopped

plain (all-purpose) flour, for coating

4 eggs, lightly beaten

dried white breadcrumbs, preferably Japanese 'panko' breadcrumbs

vegetable oil, for deep-frying

salt and ground black pepper

wedges of lemon, to garnish

side salad, to serve

Cook's Tip If the mashed potato you are using already contains butter and milk, don't add any extra or the mixture will be too soft.

1 Line a grill (broiler) pan with foil and place the fresh salmon on top. Cook under a hot grill for 2 minutes on each side, or until golden-brown on the outside, but still pink in the middle. Set aside.

2 Put the white fish and smoked haddock in a pan. Add the garlic and thyme and pour over just enough of the milk to cover. Bring to the boil, then gently simmer for 1 minute until the fish starts to cook. Turn off the heat and leave for 2 minutes, then remove the fish with a slotted spoon and leave to cool a little

3 Put the mashed potatoes, butter, herbs, mustard and egg yolks in a large bowl. Add 15ml/1 tbsp of the milk used for poaching the fish and season with salt and pepper. Mix well.

4 Carefully break the grilled and poached fish into large flakes, checking for and removing any bones. Add to the potato with the smoked salmon and mix together.

5 Put the flour, eggs and breadcrumbs into shallow dishes. Take about 50g/2oz of the mixture at a time and form into small croquettes, about 7.5cm/3in long. Dip each one into the flour, then the beaten egg. Dust with flour again, then beaten egg, then roll in the breadcrumbs. Chill for at least 30 minutes.

6 Half-fill a heavy pan or deep-fat fryer with oil and heat to 170°C/340°F. Fry the croquettes a few at a time for 2–3 minutes, until crisp and golden, turning so they brown evenly.

7 Drain on sheets of kitchen paper to blot up excess oil, and serve hot with a side salad, garnished with lemon wedges.

Energy 579kcal/2419kJ; Protein 44g; Carbohydrate 25g, of which sugars 7g; Fat 35g, of which saturates 10g; Cholesterol 416mg; Calcium 260mg; Fibre 2g; Sodium 1136mg.

Beef croquettes
Croquetas de carne

These croquettes would originally have been made from leftover meat and vegetables from a previous meal and served as a side dish rather than a main course. The soaked bread keeps the croquettes beautifully moist and also makes the meat go further.

1 Break the bread into small pieces and place in a large bowl. Sprinkle over the milk, stir to coat, and leave to soak.

2 Meanwhile, heat the olive oil in a frying pan and cook the onion over a low heat for 5 minutes, stirring occasionally until soft. Add the garlic, cumin and paprika and cook for a further 1–2 minutes, stirring frequently. Tip the mixture into the bowl and leave to cool.

3 Stir the mustard into the onions, then add the soaked bread and milk, mashing with a fork to break up the bread. Add the beef, chopped eggs, olives and parsley to the bowl. Season generously with salt and pepper.

4 Mix together thoroughly, using your hands, until combined. Divide the mixture into 24, then use your hands to shape into balls. Pour the breadcrumbs on to a large place, and roll each ball in the breadcrumbs to coat.

5 Half-fill a heavy pan or deep-fat fryer with oil and heat to 170°C/340°F.

6 Deep-fry the croquettes a few at a time for 2–3 minutes, or until crisp and golden, turning frequently so that they brown evenly. Remove the croquettes with a slotted spoon and drain on sheets of kitchen paper to blot up excess oil. Serve while still hot and crispy.

Serves 4

2 slices white bread, crusts removed

45ml/3 tbsp milk

30ml/2 tbsp olive oil

1 onion, finely chopped

2 cloves garlic, finely chopped

2.5ml/$\frac{1}{2}$ tsp ground cumin

2.5ml/$\frac{1}{2}$ tsp ground paprika

2.5ml/$\frac{1}{2}$ tsp mustard

500g/1$\frac{1}{4}$lb/4$\frac{1}{4}$ cups lean minced (ground) beef

2 hard-boiled eggs, chopped

6 pitted green olives, finely chopped

15ml/1 tbsp chopped fresh parsley

dried breadcrumbs, to coat

vegetable oil, for deep-frying

salt and ground black pepper

Energy 503kcal/2098kJ; Protein 34g; Carbohydrate 17g, of which sugars 3g; Fat 34g, of which saturates 9g; Cholesterol 169mg; Calcium 80mg; Fibre 2g; Sodium 294mg.

Courgette-flower fritters
Buñuelos de flores de zapallo

Once a dish eaten mostly by the poor, who made use of every available ingredient, these fritters are now regarded as a delicacy and much enjoyed during the very short season in which they are in bloom. Delicate and tender courgette flowers are coated in a light batter and shallow-fried until golden and crisp.

1 Whisk the eggs and milk in a bowl. Add the parsley and nutmeg and season to taste with salt and pepper. Sift over the flour and whisk well, until you have a smooth batter.

2 Pour the oil into a heavy pan and heat to 180°C/350°C. Dip the courgette flowers into the batter, then drop into the oil. Cook two or three at a time, turning so they brown evenly.

3 When dark-golden brown, lift the courgette-flowers out of the pan with a slotted spoon and drain on kitchen paper.

4 In a bowl, stir together 60ml/4 tbsp Greek yogurt, two finely sliced spring onions, a little finely chopped fresh red chilli, to taste, and a pinch of salt. Serve the fritters hot, dipped in the yogurt.

Serves 4

2 eggs

90ml/6 tbsp milk

15ml/1 tbsp chopped fresh parsley

1.5ml/¼ tsp freshly ground nutmeg

115g/4oz/½ cup self-raising (self-rising) flour

12 courgette (zucchini) flowers

about 250ml/8fl oz/1 cup olive oil

salt and ground black pepper

Greek (US strained plain) yogurt, spring onions (scallions) and fresh red chillies, to serve

Energy 414kcal/1720kJ; Protein 7g; Carbohydrate 23g, of which sugars 1g; Fat 34g, of which saturates 5g; Cholesterol 119mg; Calcium 127mg; Fibre 2g; Sodium 148mg.

Grilled provolone cheese
Provoleta

Serves 4

4 provolone cheese slices,
  each about 5cm/2in thick

30–45ml/3–4 tbsp olive oil

5ml/1 tsp dried oregano

1.5ml/¼ tsp dried chilli flakes

sea salt and ground black
  pepper

slices of bread and
  chimichurri sauce, to serve

This warm cheese dish is served as a pre-meat course at most asados. Provoleta is a semi-hard cheese made in Argentina from full-fat cow's milk and shaped into a cylinder. It has a slightly 'sharp' flavour and is excellent for grilling as it becomes soft in the centre, yet still holds its shape.

1 Place the cheese on a board and lightly brush one side with the oil. Sprinkle evenly with half the oregano and chilli flakes. Turn over the slices and brush the other side with oil and the remaining oregano and chilli flakes.

2 Brush a ridged grill (broiler) pan or barbecue rack with oil and heat until very hot. Add the cheese and cook for 1–2 minutes or until golden brown. Turn over with a metal spatula and cook the other side.

3 Serve on warmed plates and drizzle with any remaining oil. Season with salt and pepper and serve while hot, together with slices of bread and chimichurri sauce.

Cook's Tip The trick to cooking provolone is to cook long enough to soften the centre, but before the outside becomes runny. If possible, leave the cheese at room temperature for about an hour to allow the outside to dry and harden slightly, before brushing with oil.

Energy 256kcal/1058kJ; Protein 13g; Carbohydrate 0g, of which sugars 0g; Fat 23g, of which saturates 11g; Cholesterol 43mg; Calcium 387mg; Fibre 0g; Sodium 463mg.

Beef pasties
Empanadas

Popular party fare, these are always served at festivals such as Revolution Day on 25th May. Although readily available from many bakeries and take-aways, they are often home-made with a lard or beef dripping dough. Traditionally deep-fried, they may be oven-baked for a healthier option.

Makes 12

For the dough

50g/2oz/¼ cup lard or white vegetable fat (shortening)

250ml/8fl oz/1 cup warm water

500g/1¼lb/4½ cups plain (all-purpose) flour

1 egg, lightly beaten, to brush

For the filling

30ml/2 tbsp lard

1 onion, finely chopped

6 spring onions (scallions), thinly sliced

2 garlic cloves, chopped

500g/1¼lb lean beef, cut into 1cm/½in cubes

15ml/1 tbsp ground paprika

5ml/1 tsp ground cumin

5ml/1 tsp dried chilli flakes

4 hard-boiled eggs, roughly chopped

115g/4oz/1 cup pitted green olives, chopped

salt

1 Cut the lard into small cubes, add to the water and leave until melted. Sift the flour and a pinch of salt into a bowl, make a hollow in the middle and add the lard and water. Mix together to make a smooth dough. Wrap in plastic wrap and leave at room temperature for at least an hour.

2 Meanwhile, make the filling. Melt the lard in a large frying pan and fry the onion for 5 minutes, until soft. Add the spring onions, garlic and beef and cook for 3–4 minutes or until the meat is brown. Add the spices and cook for 2 minutes.

3 Remove the pan from the heat and leave to cool. Stir in the eggs and olives and season to taste with salt. Set aside.

4 Divide the dough into 12 even-sized pieces and roll out each (one at a time) on a lightly floured surface to a circle 12–15cm/4½–6in.

5 Divide the filling among the dough rounds, piling it into the centre. Lightly brush the edges with beaten egg. Fold over to make a half-moon shape, and press the edges together.

6 Half-fill a heavy pan or deep-fat fryer with oil and heat to 170°C/340°F. Fry the empanadas one or two at time until a deep golden-brown.

7 Remove with a slotted spoon and drain on kitchen paper. Bring the fat up to temperature before cooking another batch. Alternatively, preheat the oven to 200°C/400°F/Gas 6. Glaze the empanadas with the beaten egg, and bake for 10 minutes, then reduce the temperature to 180°C/350°F/Gas 4 and bake for a further 15–20 minutes.

8 Serve the empanadas hot or cool on a wire rack and eat at room temperature.

Cook's Tip Both the pastry and filling can be made in advance and chilled in the refrigerator until needed. Stack the circles of dough using baking parchment inbetween each layer, and cover with plastic wrap or baking parchment. Remove from the refrigerator 15 minutes before shaping and cooking.

The filled empanadas can also be stored in the refrigerator for up to a day before cooking.

Energy 297kcal/1248kJ; Protein 16g; Carbohydrate 34g, of which sugars2g; Fat 12g, of which saturates 4g; Cholesterol 116mg; Calcium 87mg; Fibre 2g; Sodium 154mg.

Spanish omelette
Tortilla

Spain's famous tapa is much-enjoyed in Argentina. Made from a few simple ingredients – usually eggs, potatoes and onions – it is cooked like a flat omelette and served hot or cold, cut into thick wedges. All kinds of extra vegetables, cooked meats and flavourings can be added.

1 Heat 15ml/1 tbsp of the oil in a heavy non-stick frying pan about 25cm/10in diameter.

2 Add the chopped onion and garlic to the pan and cook over a medium heat until softened. Transfer to a large bowl with a slotted spoon, leaving any fat behind in the pan.

3 Add the remaining 30ml/2 tbsp oil to the pan, then add the potatoes and cook until golden-brown and soft in the middle when pierced with a sharp knife. Allow the potatoes to cool for a few minutes.

4 Add the eggs and cream to the bowl with the onions and whisk together with a fork. Season generously with plenty of salt and pepper. Add the potatoes. and stir gently.

5 Wipe the frying pan clean, then add the butter to the pan and heat until melted and bubbling. Pour the egg and potato mixture into the pan, pushing the potato slices so they are flat and evenly distributed. Cook for around 3–4 minutes or until the egg has set on the base and is golden brown.

6 Place a large plate upside down on top of the pan, invert the pan, holding the plate with your other hand, so that the tortilla flips onto the plate. Slide the tortilla back into the pan, with the cooked, golden brown side upwards.

7 Cook the tortilla for a few minutes more, then slide from the pan on to a clean plate. Allow to cool for 10 minutes. Cut into wedges and serve warm, or at room temperature.

Cook's Tip If you prefer, the top of the tortilla can be cooked under a preheated hot grill (broiler) to set and brown the top.

Variations
• For a spinach tortilla, replace the potatoes with 350g/12oz well-drained cooked and chopped spinach and 2.5ml/1/2 tsp freshly grated nutmeg, mixing in with the onions and beaten eggs.
• For a spicy tortilla, add a chopped Spanish chorizo sausage when cooking the onion; add just a tiny amount of oil to the pan to start the cooking and use the fat from the chorizo to cook the potatoes.

Serves 4

45ml/3 tbsp olive oil

1 onion, finely chopped

2 garlic cloves, thinly sliced

3 large potatoes, peeled and cut into thin slices

25g/1oz/2 tbsp butter, preferably unsalted (sweet)

4–5 large eggs

50ml/2fl oz/1/4 cup double (heavy) cream

salt and ground black pepper

Energy 398kcal/1657kJ; Protein 13g; Carbohydrate 29g, of which sugars 3g; Fat 27g, of which saturates 8g; Cholesterol 310mg; Calcium 65mg; Fibre 3g; Sodium 119mg.

Zapallito tart
Tarta de zapallito

Tarts are the big brothers of empanadas and hugely popular with Argentinians, and this recipe is probably the country's favourite. Zapallito are summer squash with dark green skins and orange flesh. They are similar in taste to courgettes, but with a sweeter flavour and denser texture.

Serves 8–12

For the pastry

400g/14oz/3½ cups plain (all-purpose) flour

pinch of salt

50g/2oz/¼ cup butter, softened

1 egg

60–75ml/4–5 tbsp water

beaten egg, to glaze

For the filling

40g/1½oz/3 tbsp butter

2 onions, chopped

500g/1¼lb zapallito or courgettes (zucchini), cut into 2cm/¾in dice

1 red (bell) pepper, seeded and chopped

115g/4oz/1⅓ cups grated Parmesan

3 eggs

200ml/7fl oz/scant 1 cup double (heavy) cream

salt and ground black pepper

tomato, onion and rocket (arugula) salad, to serve

1 Sift the flour and salt together in a mound on a marble slab, pastry board or cold work surface. Make a well in the centre and put in the butter, egg and a few tablespoons of water.

2 Using your fingertips and thumbs only, work the butter, egg, and water together until the mixture resembles scrambled eggs. As you do this, pull in a little of the surrounding flour to prevent the mixture from becoming too sticky.

3 When the mixture begins to form a smooth paste, pull in more of the flour to make a dough, gradually working in all the flour. If the pastry is slightly crumbly at this stage, work in a little extra water. Lightly knead the dough briefly until smooth, then cover with plastic wrap and leave it to rest for 30 minutes at room temperature.

4 For the filling, melt the butter in a large pan and cook the onion for 3–4 minutes or until beginning to soften. Add the zapallito or courgettes, cover and cook for 3–4 minutes, then uncover the pan, add the pepper and continue cooking for 5–6 minutes or until the vegetables are tender and most of the liquid has evaporated. Leave to cool.

5 Put the eggs and cream in a bowl and whisk together to combine, then stir in the Parmesan, followed by the cooked vegetables. Season to taste with salt and pepper. Put a baking sheet in the oven. Preheat to 180°C/350°F/Gas 4.

6 Roll out slightly more than half of the pastry and use to line a 24cm/9½in diameter, 3cm/1¼in deep, fluted flan tin (pan). Spoon in the filling into the case, then roll out the remaining pastry, dampen the edges and place over the pie. Trim the edges with a knife.

7 Glaze the top of the pie with beaten egg and make a few small holes in the top. Place on the hot baking sheet and bake for 15 minutes.

8 Lower the temperature to 160°C/325°F/Gas 3 and bake the tart for 15–25 minutes more. Leave to cool for a few minutes or serve at room temperature before cutting and serving with a tomato, onion and rocket salad.

Cook's Tip Although rarely available in shops and supermarkets, it is possible to buy zapillito seeds and grow your own.

Energy 314kcal/1310kJ; Protein 11g; Carbohydrate 28g, of which sugars 2g; Fat 19g, of which saturates 10g; Cholesterol 135mg; Calcium 179mg; Fibre 1g; Sodium 137mg.

Beef pie
Pastel de papas

Serves 6

30ml/2 tbsp olive oil

2 onions, finely chopped

1 red (bell) pepper, seeded and chopped

1 red chilli, seeded and finely chopped

2 cloves garlic, finely chopped

500g/1¼lb/2 cups minced (ground) beef

2 tomatoes, roughly chopped

5ml/1 tsp ground paprika

100ml/3½fl oz/scant ½ cup stock or water

100g/4oz/1 cup green olives

4 hard-boiled eggs, chopped

800g/1¾lb/10½ cups cooked, mashed potatoes

3 eggs, lightly beaten

5ml/1 tsp grated nutmeg

115g/4oz/1⅓ cups grated Parmesan

salt and ground black pepper

This comforting cold-weather dish has layers of minced beef and creamy mashed potatoes and is similar to British cottage pie. Other countries may lay claim to this dish, but Argentinians are convinced it is their own creation.

1 Heat the oil in a large frying pan and fry the onion for 5 minutes. Add the red pepper, chilli and garlic and cook for 3–4 minutes until tender. Transfer into a bowl and set aside.

2 Brown the beef over a high heat, stirring. Return the vegetables to the pan, add the tomatoes and paprika and stock and bring to the boil. Cover, reduce the heat and simmer for 20 minutes. Remove the lid and simmer for a further 10 minutes until the mixture is fairly dry. Preheat the oven to 180°C/350°F/Gas 4.

3 Remove from the heat and stir in the olives, chopped eggs and salt and pepper.

4 Mix the mashed potatoes, with the eggs, nutmeg and half of the Parmesan. In a large ovenproof dish, layer up the beef and the potato mixtures alternately; there should be at least two layers of each. Finish with potatoes.

5 Sprinkle the remaining Parmesan over the top and bake for 35–40 minutes or until piping hot and the top is golden-brown.

Energy 503kcal/2105kJ; Protein 37g; Carbohydrate 30g, of which sugars 7g; Fat 27g, of which saturates 10g; Cholesterol 312mg; Calcium 271mg; Fibre 4g; Sodium 589mg.

Corn parcels
Tamales de humita

This corn dish is enjoyed in the north of the country where the largest numbers of Amerindian communities live. Tamales originated in Central America, but the Argentinian version is milder and less spicy.

1 Melt the butter in a pan, add the onion and cook over a medium heat for 7–8 minutes, until softened, stirring frequently. Add the corn, spring onions, red pepper, paprika and 45ml/ 3 tbsp water. Cover and cook for 10 minutes or until the vegetables are very soft.

2 Blend half the mixture in a food processor or with a hand blender, until smooth. Stir in the rest of the corn mixture and leave to cool.

3 Bring a pan of water to the boil and blanch the leaves for 1 minute to soften. Transfer to a colander and leave to drain and cool a little.

4 Stir the cheese into the corn mixture and season. Place the corn leaves on a board and divide the mixture between them.

5 Fold in the ends and sides of the corn leaves over the mixture, making a neat parcel and making sure that all the filling is enclosed. Tie the parcels with string.

6 Put the parcels in a steamer over the pan of boiling water and steam for 30–35 minutes. Allow the parcels to cool a little, before cutting the string and unwrapping them. Serve with chilli sauce to drizzle over.

Serves 4

50g/2oz/¼ cup butter

1 onion, finely chopped

500g/1¼lb/6½ cups canned corn kernels

3 spring onions (scallions), sliced

1 red (bell) pepper, seeded and finely diced

1.5ml/¼ tsp ground paprika

8 large corn leaves

115g/4oz mozzarella cheese, cut into small dice

salt and ground black pepper

chilli sauce, to serve

Energy 348kcal/1489kJ; Protein 10g; Carbohydrate 39g, of which sugars 17g; Fat 18g, of which saturates g; Cholesterol 43mg; Calcium 134mg; Fibre 6g; Sodium 531mg.

Chickpea flat bread
Fainá

This simple unleavened bread is made with gram flour, a pale yellow powdery flour, made from chickpeas, that has a mild earthy flavour. Slices of fainá are often served alongside pizza, and Argentinians enjoy a slice of this placed on top of a slice of pizza and eaten together like a sandwich.

1 Put the gram flour in a bowl, and pour in the water and oil. Using a balloon or electric whisk, mix until the batter is smooth and lump-free. Season with salt and pepper. Cover the bowl with plastic wrap and chill for 2 hours.

2 Preheat the oven to 240°C/475°F/Gas 9. Lightly oil a 33cm/14in pizza pan or a 28 x 38cm/11 x 15in baking tray.

3 Place the baking tray in the oven to heat for 2 minutes, then remove from the oven and pour in the batter in an even layer.

4 Bake for 10–15 minutes or until lightly browned. Leave to stand for a few minutes, then carefully remove the flat bread from the baking tray, and drizzle with a little extra olive oil. Serve warm.

Serves 4–8

300g/11oz/2¼ cups gram flour

900ml/1½ pints/3¾ cups water

50ml/2fl oz/¼ cup olive oil, plus extra for greasing and drizzling

sea salt and ground black pepper

Energy 185kcal/775kJ; Protein 7g; Carbohydrate 19g, of which sugars 1g; Fat 10g, of which saturates 1g; Cholesterol 0mg; Calcium 68mg; Fibre 5g; Sodium 15mg.

Potato gnocchi
Ñoquis del 29

Serves 4

500g/1¼lb waxy potatoes, scrubbed

25g/1oz/2 tbsp butter

2 egg yolks

5ml/1 tsp freshly grated nutmeg

30ml/2 tbsp grated Parmesan

pinch of salt

160g/5½oz/1⅓ cups plain (all-purpose) flour

tomato sauce (see page 26)

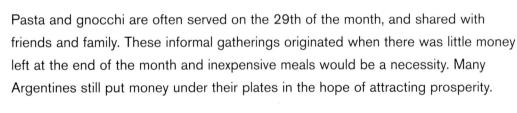

Pasta and gnocchi are often served on the 29th of the month, and shared with friends and family. These informal gatherings originated when there was little money left at the end of the month and inexpensive meals would be a necessity. Many Argentines still put money under their plates in the hope of attracting prosperity.

1 Place the unpeeled potatoes in a large pan of water. Bring to the boil and cook until tender but not falling apart.

2 Drain the potatoes, and peel when cool enough to handle. Mash with the butter until smooth, then stir in the egg yolks, nutmeg, Parmesan and a pinch of salt.

3 Sift over the flour and mix into the potatoes. Don't overwork the dough or the ñoquis won't be light and fluffy. Cover the dough and leave to rest for 30 minutes, then divide in two.

4 On a lightly floured board, form each section into a roll about 2.5cm/1in in diameter. Cut the rolls into pieces about 2.5cm/1in long. One by one, press and roll the gnocchi lightly along the tines of a fork, making ridges on one side and a depression from your thumb on the other.

5 Bring a large pan of salted water to a rapid boil. Drop the gnocchi in, in batches. When the gnocchi rise to the surface, lift out with a slotted spoon and place in a warm serving dish. Serve with hot tomato sauce, topped with shavings of Parmesan, if you wish.

Energy 322kcal/1356kJ; Protein 9g; Carbohydrate 51g, of which sugars 2g; Fat 10g, of which saturates 5g; Cholesterol 119mg; Calcium 128mg; Fibre 3g; Sodium 95mg.

Fish and Shellfish

Many species of fish and shellfish are abundant in the waters of Argentina's coasts and rivers, although much of the catch is exported. Fish is cooked quickly and simply in Spanish-influenced dishes.

Coastal and inland waters rich in fish

In a country that is among the world's leaders in meat production, fish is seen as secondary. In fact, fisherman from Japan and Taiwan travel all the way to Argentina from Asia to cast their nets in its relatively unpopulated waters, which are kept cool by streams from Antarctica. In the past fish was what was eaten when you had to, during the times when the Catholic church forbids the consumption of meat, which perhaps explains the negative attitude.

Patagonia enjoys trout, however, from its inland waters; Ushuaia, the world's most southerly city, is famous for its king crab; Rosario has some lovely river-facing restaurants, serving up fish from the Paraná; and coastal resorts have beach cafés selling freshly caught and cooked seafood such as fried whitebait.

Typical fish dishes include whole fish baked in sea salt, white fish fillets cooked in the Milanesa style – coated in breadcrumbs and fried – while prawns (shrimp) are often served with salad as an appetizer or first course. Smaller fish are often quickly fried, either in a light batter or in flour, and served with lemon wedges and crusty bread. Southern king crab fished on the Pacific coast is a great favourite, and is often mixed with mayonnaise and served on hot toast.

Right middle: The freshwater lakes of Patagonia.

Fish milanesas
Milanesas de pescado

Serves 4

4 fish fillets such as sea bass or bream, each weighing about 200g/7oz, boned and skinned

50g/2oz/½ cup plain (all-purpose) flour

115g/4oz/2 cups dry white breadcrumbs

2 eggs, lightly beaten

15ml/1 tbsp chopped fresh parsley

vegetable oil, for deep-frying

sea salt and ground black pepper

lemon wedges, to garnish

chips (fries) and seasonal vegetables, to serve

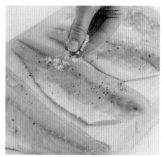

Milanesas, deep-fried fillets, are an Argentinian favourite; traditionally a thin beef or veal steak, coated with herby breadcrumbs, then fried until crisp and golden. This fish version is especially popular at Easter, when many refrain from eating meat.

1 Pat the fish fillets dry on kitchen paper, then season on both sides with salt and pepper.

2 Place the flour and breadcrumbs on separate plates. Put the eggs and parsley in a shallow dish and lightly whisk together with a fork.

3 Dip each fish fillet in the flour and shake off the excess, dip in the egg, then in the flour again, then back in the egg and finally in the breadcrumbs. Place on a tray lined with baking parchment and chill for at least 20 minutes.

4 Half-fill a deep-fat fryer or heavy pan with oil and heat to 170°C/340°F. Fry the fish, two fillets at a time for 5–6 minutes or until golden-brown and cooked through.

5 Drain on kitchen paper and keep warm while cooking the second batch. Garnish with lemon and serve with chips and seasonal vegetables.

Cook's tip If the fillets are very thick, remove from the pan when golden brown and finish cooking in an oven at 180°C/350°F/Gas 4.

Energy 470kcal/1977kJ; Protein 43g; Carbohydrate 32g, of which sugars 1g; Fat 20g, of which saturates 2g; Cholesterol 195mg; Calcium 153mg; Fibre 2g; Sodium 482mg.

Salt-baked fish
Dorado a la sal

Dorado are huge river fish which come from the tropical regions of Argentina and can weigh as much as 65kg/150lb. They have beautiful gold-coloured skins and firm, slightly oily meat. Sea bass, used here, is a good substitute.

1 Put the salt in a bowl with the herbs and add 45ml/3 tbsp tablespoons of water. Stir until evenly mixed.

2 Preheat the oven to 200°C/400°F/Gas 6. Squeeze the lemon juice over both sides of the fish, then place the squeezed lemon halves in the cavity of the fish.

3 Spread out half of the damp salt mixture on a shallow baking tray.

4 Place the fish on top of the salt. Pour the remaining salt on top of the fish, then mould the salt all around the fish, pressing it down, making sure it is completely covered.

5 Bake for 45 minutes to 1 hour (the fish will be done when the salt crust dries out). Carefully remove all the salt crust before transferring the fish to a plate and peeling off the skin. Garnish with fresh herbs and lemon wedges to squeeze over the fish.

Serves 4–6

2kg/4½lb rough sea salt or rock salt

½ bunch fresh thyme leaves

½ bunch fresh dill, chopped

½ bunch parsley, chopped

2kg/4½lb dorado, sea bass, or similar whole fish, scaled and gutted

2 lemons, halved

ground black pepper

fresh herbs and lemon wedges, to garnish

Energy 368kcal/1545kJ; Protein 60g; Carbohydrate 1g, of which sugars 1g; Fat 14g, of which saturates 3g; Cholesterol 137mg; Calcium 33mg; Fibre 1g; Sodium 759mg.

Seafood stew
Cazuela de mariscos

Argentina has a long coastline and numerous rivers where fish and shellfish are abundant. This tasty dish – a cross between a thick soup and a stew – is recognizable as being Spanish in origin, and is full of peppers, tomatoes and a range of seafood; choose whatever is available and in peak season.

1 Heat the olive oil in a large pan, add the chopped onions and cook for 2–3 minutes, then add the red pepper and garlic and cook for a further 3–4 minutes over a medium heat, until the pepper has softened.

2 Add the bay leaf, saffron and paprika to the pan, then pour in the wine or vermouth. Stir for a few minutes, and bring to a rapid boil.

3 Add the mussels to the pan and immediately cover with a lid. Cook for 3–4 minutes, shaking the pan gently half way through cooking, until the mussels have opened. Remove the mussels with a slotted spoon, discarding any which haven't opened. Set aside.

4 Add the tomatoes, fish stock and sliced squid to the pan. Cover, and on a low heat simmer very gently for 10 minutes.

5 Add the whole langoustines or prawns, and the cooked octopus to the pan, and simmer for a further 5 minutes untill the langoustines have turned pink.

6 Return the mussels to the pan with the peas, parsley and the squeezed juice from ½ lemon. Season to taste with salt and pepper and heat until piping hot. Serve straight away with crusty bread and the remaining 1½ lemons, cut into wedges, to garnish.

Serves 4–6

30ml/2 tbsp olive oil

2 onions, chopped

1 red (bell) pepper, seeded and diced

3 garlic cloves, chopped

1 bay leaf

pinch of saffron strands

5ml/1 tsp paprika

120ml/4fl oz/½ cup dry white wine or vermouth

200g/7oz prepared fresh mussels

4 tomatoes, chopped

250ml/8fl oz/1 cup fish stock

4 fresh squid tubes, cleaned and sliced

12 fresh langoustines or large prawns (jumbo shrimp), whole, unshelled

1 small octopus, cooked in boiling water for 30 minutes per kg and cut into bitesize pieces

150g/5oz/1¼ cups cooked peas

small bunch fresh parsley, chopped

2 lemons

sea salt and ground black pepper

crusty bread, to serve

Energy 344kcal/1452kJ; Protein 53g; Carbohydrate 11g, of which sugars 11g; Fat 8g, of which saturates 2g; Cholesterol 340mg; Calcium 112mg; Fibre 3g; Sodium 394mg.

Fried whitebait
Cornalitos fritos

Whitebait are tiny immature fish, usually herring, which are typically deep-fried and eaten whole. They are a classic quick summer snack, often served at beach cafés in Mar del Plata and invariably enjoyed with an ice-cold beer.

1 Rinse the whitebait in a colander under cold running water. Pat dry with kitchen paper, and season with salt and pepper.

2 Sift the flour in a bowl, then add the lager or water and eggs and mix together with a whisk or hand-held blender to make a smooth batter.

3 Half-fill a heavy pan or deep-fat fryer with oil and heat to 180°C/350°F.

4 Coat the fish, a few at a time, in the batter, then drop into the hot oil. Cook in batches for 2–3 minutes or until dark golden and crisp. Lift out of the oil and drain on kitchen paper. Make sure the oil comes back up to temperature before adding the next batch.

5 For the tartare sauce, mix all the ingredients together in a small bowl. Serve the fish while still hot, together with the sauce.

Serves 4

600g/1lb 6oz whitebait

200g/7oz/scant 2 cups plain (all-purpose) flour

200ml/7fl oz/scant 1 cup cold lager or sparkling water

2 eggs, lightly beaten

salt and ground black pepper

For the tartare sauce

120ml/4fl oz/½ cup fresh mayonnaise

30ml/2 tbsp gherkins, finely chopped

15ml/1 tbsp capers, chopped

1 small shallot, finely chopped

15ml/1 tbsp chopped fresh parsley

15ml/1 tbsp lemon juice

Energy 866kcal/3580kJ; Protein 25g; Carbohydrate 8g, of which sugars 1g; Fat 82g, of which saturates 3g; Cholesterol 23mg; Calcium 1081mg; Fibre 0g; Sodium 423mg.

King crab toasts
Tostadas de centolla

Serves 4

1 red chilli, seeded and finely chopped

1 lime, halved

2 spring onions (scallions) finely sliced

15ml/1 tbsp mayonnaise

15ml/1 tbsp crème fraîche

15ml/1 tbsp chopped fresh coriander (cilantro), plus extra to garnish

dash Tabasco sauce

350g/12oz white crab meat

50g/2oz brown crab meat

4 slices sourdough bread, toasted

sea salt

King crabs are caught in the waters off Tierra del Fuego in the most southern part of Argentina, some growing as large as 6kg/13lb. This recipe makes use of both the white and brown meat for maximum taste.

1 Put the red chilli in a bowl and squeeze over the juice from half the lime. Add the spring onions, mayonnaise, crème fraîche, chopped coriander, Tabasco sauce and sea salt to taste.

2 Pick over and flake the crab meat, discarding any fragments of shell, and add to the sauce.

3 Gently fold the crab into the sauce, taking care not to break up the crab meat too much.

4 Toast the slices of sourdough and divide the crab meat mixture between the slices. Garnish with a sprinkling of chopped coriander and the remaining lime half, cut into thin wedges.

Energy 218kcal/915kJ; Protein 18g; Carbohydrate 18g, of which sugars 2g; Fat 9g, of which saturates 2g; Cholesterol 61mg; Calcium 47mg; Fibre 2g; Sodium 522mg.

Trout with orange and herbs
Trucha con hierbas y naranja

Serves 4

4 small trout, about 275g/10oz each, cleaned

4 oranges

60ml/4 tbsp olive oil

½ bunch fresh dill

½ bunch fresh thyme

few sprigs of fresh rosemary

few sprigs of fresh parsley

sea salt and ground black pepper

rocket (arugula), beetroot (beet) and toasted almond salad, and crusty bread and butter, to serve

People come from all over the world on fishing trips to try their luck catching wild trout in the cold-water rivers in the south of Argentina. Fragrant oranges and herbs enhance the delicate flavour of the fish in this simple recipe.

1 Preheat the oven to 180°C/350°F/Gas 4. Make three diagonal cuts on each side of the fish. Cut two of the oranges in half, place cut side down, then cut each half into six slices. Season the fish well, inside and out and then put a slice of orange into each incision.

2 Light oil a baking sheet, then arrange half the herbs over the tray. Place the fish on top, then scatter the rest of the herbs over. Drizzle with the rest of the oil.

3 Cut the remaining two oranges in half and squeeze out the juice. Pour over the fish. Bake for 25–30 minutes or until the fish is just cooked and tender.

4 Remove the herbs from the top of the fish, and cut the head off, if you wish.

5 Arrange the rocket, beetroot and almond salad on four plates and place a fish on top of each. Serve with crusty bread and butter.

Energy 459kcal/1922kJ; Protein 41g; Carbohydrate 17g, of which sugars 17g; Fat 26g, of which saturates 4g; Cholesterol 134mg; Calcium 130mg; Fibre 4g; Sodium 100mg.

Salmon ceviche with pink grapefruit and avocado
Ceviche de salmon con pomelo rosado y palta

This is a fantastic dish for hot summer days as no cooking is involved. Ceviche – 'cooking' the fish in citrus juices – is often made with white fish, but here fresh salmon is used. Serve as a light lunch for four, or as an appetizer for six people.

1 Put the salmon on a tray or large plate and lightly sprinkle with salt. Cover and chill in the refrigerator for 20 minutes.

2 Meanwhile, working over a bowl to catch the juices, peel the grapefruit and cut between the membranes to cut out the segments, dropping them into the bowl. Squeeze the juice from the membranes into the bowl.

3 Add to the bowl the juice of 1 1/2 limes, the sugar, jalapeño, and Tabasco to taste. Mix well.

4 Halve the avocado, peel and chop the flesh, then purée in a food processor with the juice from the remaining half lime.

5 Remove the salmon from the refrigerator, rinse and dry. Freeze for 5–10 minutes, then slice very thinly and arrange on a plate.

6 Arrange the grapefruit segments over the fish and spoon some of the dressing on top (serve the rest separately). Finish the dish with drops of avocado purée and coriander leaves.

Serves 4–6

500g/1 1/4lb very fresh salmon, boned and skinned

1 pink grapefruit

2 limes

5ml/1 tsp caster (superfine) sugar

1 jalapeño pepper, finely chopped

dash Tabasco sauce

1 ripe avocado

salt

fresh coriander (cilantro), to garnish

Cook's tip If preparing in advance, cover the sliced dressed salmon and refrigerate. Remove about half an hour before serving to allow it to come to room temperature. Spoon over the grapefruit, and avocado just before serving.

Energy 227kcal/944kJ; Protein 18g; Carbohydrate 4g, of which sugars 4g; Fat 16g, of which saturates 3g; Cholesterol 42mg; Calcium 33mg; Fibre 1g; Sodium 44mg.

Meat, Poultry and Game

Argentinians are famous for eating beef, but their love of meat also extends to pork, lamb, chicken and offal, and they will happily consume a huge variety in just one meal.

Quantity, variety, but above all quality

High-quality meat is not a luxury in Argentina, it is seen as a staple, available to almost every budget. Argentine beef and its production have played a major part in the culture, from the asado to the history of the gauchos of the Pampas. Landowners became wealthy from beef production and export, and estancia owners built large houses, important buildings in Buenos Aires and elsewhere, and contributed to politics, philanthropy and society. The agricultural show La Rural each winter in Buenos Aires has been a major part of the social season since it started in 1886.

The asado, of course, is where beef is most highly valued, but at the same time kidneys, sausages, pork, lamb, and sometimes chicken is also grilled, so that every guest has as much of each kind of meat as they want. Meat is also used in pasta dishes; joints of beef, lamb and pork are stuffed, rolled and roasted; and thin fillets of the best cuts are often cooked 'milanesa', coated in egg and breadcrumbs and fried until crispy and golden. Hearty stews and casseroles are also a favourite, often slow cooking economical cuts until tender or made with the offal – especially tripe and sweetbreads – that Argentinians love.

Right middle: Three gauchos, the Argentinian cattle herders of the Pampas, instantly identifiable by their iconic red cloaks.

Chicken in blue cheese sauce
Pollo al Roquefort

Roquefort is a crumbly white cheese with blue-green veins. Traditionally made from unpasteurized ewe's milk, the technique was introduced to Argentina by the French who settled there. It is now one of the most popular cheeses in the country.

1 Skin the chicken breast fillets, then season with salt and pepper and lightly dust with the flour. Heat the oil and butter in a large frying pan until the butter is foaming. Add the chicken and cook for 7–8 minutes, turning once, until it is golden-brown. Remove from the pan, leaving the fat and juices behind, and set aside.

2 Add the onions and garlic to the pan and fry for 4–5 minutes, stirring frequently. Pour in the wine and add the bay leaf and thyme. Bring to the boil and simmer for a minute.

3 Stir in the chicken stock and milk, then return the chicken to the pan. Cover with a lid and cook over a low heat for 15 minutes.

4 Add the blue cheese and cream and mix until the cheese has melted. Cover and cook for a further 20–25 minutes, or until the chicken is tender and cooked through and the sauce has thickened. Just before serving, squeeze over the juice of half a lemon and sprinkle with chopped parsley. Serve with steamed potatoes and asparagus or green beans.

Serves 4

4 chicken breast fillets, each weighing about 250g/9oz

60ml/4 tbsp flour

30ml/2 tbsp olive oil

25g/1oz/2 tbsp butter

2 onions, chopped

2 cloves garlic, halved

120ml/4fl oz/½ cup white wine

1 bay leaf

a few sprigs of fresh thyme

120ml/4fl oz/½ cup chicken stock

250ml/8fl oz/1 cup whole milk

250g/9oz blue cheese, such as Roquefort, crumbled

250ml/8fl oz/1 cup double (heavy) cream

salt and ground black pepper

½ lemon

chopped parsley, to garnish

steamed vegetables, to serve

Energy 1046kcal/4350kJ; Protein 78g; Carbohydrate 22g, of which sugars 9g; Fat 72g, of which saturates 40g; Cholesterol 339mg; Calcium 492mg; Fibre 2g; Sodium 1316mg.

Lemon and wine glazed chicken
Pollo al limon

Serves 4

4 lemons

1 chicken, about 1.3kg/3lb

60ml/4 tbsp olive oil

2 onions, peeled and quartered

2 large leeks, cut into 2.5cm/
  1 in slices

10 garlic cloves, unpeeled

120ml/4fl oz/$\frac{1}{2}$ cup white wine

salt and ground black pepper

a few sprigs of thyme

roast potatoes and steamed
  green beans, to serve

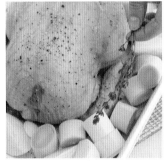

This is a simple way to roast a chicken along with caramelized onions and leeks. Use an Argentinian Chardonnay for the recipe if you can, as it has just the right fruity notes and is one of the country's favourite wines, produced extensively in Mendoza.

1 Preheat the oven to 200°C/400°F/Gas 6. Cut the lemons in half and squeeze out the juice. Push the lemon halves inside the cavity of the chicken. Put the chicken in a roasting pan and season well with salt and pepper. Cover with foil and roast for 40 minutes, then turn down the oven to 180°C/350°F/Gas 4.

2 Toss the onions, leeks and garlic in the oil. Remove the foil from the chicken and add the vegetables and thyme to the roasting pan.

3 Pour the wine and lemon juice over the chicken and cook for a further 40–45 minutes, basting with the juices every 15 minutes. The chicken is cooked when the juices run clear when a knife is inserted into the thickest part of the thigh.

4 Cover and allow to rest for 10 minutes, then carve the chicken into pieces or slices. Serve with the roasted vegetables, roast potatoes and steamed green beans.

Energy 542kcal/2261kJ; Protein 57g; Carbohydrate 10g, of which sugars 6g; Fat 31g, of which saturates 6g; Cholesterol 210mg; Calcium 62mg; Fibre 3g; Sodium 164mg.

Veal milanesas
Milanesas de ternera

Serves 4

4 veal escalopes, weighing
150–175g/5–6oz each

2 eggs, lightly beaten

30ml/2 tbsp chopped fresh
parsley

2 garlic cloves, crushed

plain (all-purpose) flour, for
dusting

dry white breadcrumbs

vegetable oil for deep-frying

salt and ground black pepper

lemon wedges, to garnish

chips (fries) and salad, to
serve

Milanesas, thin pieces of meat, coated in breadcrumbs and fried, are as popular in Argentina as barbecued meat. They can be made with chicken breast or pork fillet, batted out to a thin steak, and are often eaten by office workers in a sandwich.

1 Pat the veal escalopes dry on kitchen paper and season with salt and pepper.

2 Mix the eggs, parsley and garlic together on a plate or shallow container. Place the flour and breadcrumbs on separate plates or containers.

3 Dip the escalopes one at a time, first in the flour, shaking off any excess, then in the egg and finally in the breadcrumbs. Put on a baking sheet, lined with baking parchment, and chill in the refrigerator for at least 30 minutes.

4 Half-fill a heavy pan or deep-fat fryer with oil and heat to 180°C/350°F. Deep-fry the escalopes one or two at a time for 3–4 minutes until deep golden and cooked through. Drain on kitchen paper before serving with chips and salad and lemon wedges to squeeze over, or in a hunk of French baguette.

Cook's Tip These can be oven-baked instead of fried, cook in a preheated oven at 200°C/400°F/Gas 6 for 10–12 minutes, turning half way through the cooking time.

Energy 312kcal/1306kJ; Protein 38g; Carbohydrate 4g, of which sugars 0g; Fat 16g, of which saturates 3g; Cholesterol 197mg; Calcium 33mg; Fibre 0g; Sodium 132mg.

Italian-style barbecued beef
Matambre a la pizza

Argentinians worship beef and adore pizza, and here is the dish that combines both, with meat, tomato and cheese. The tomato sauce helps to moisten the meat as well as adding flavour, while the mozzarella topping gives a pizza-like appearance.

1 Trim the beef, then 'butterfly' by slicing through it lengthwise, almost to the other side, then opening it like a book.

2 Put the meat between two sheets of oiled clear film (plastic wrap), outer-side facing down and with one of the longer sides towards you and gently bash with a meat mallet or rolling pin until it is an even thickness (this will help tenderize the meat).

3 Season the meat with salt and pepper, then place over a hot barbecue, or a preheated ridged griddle, for about 5 minutes or until it is well browned. Turn the meat and cover the cooked side with a good layer of tomato sauce.

4 Arrange the mozzarella on top of the sauce Continue cooking until the meat is done to your liking. Sprinkle with oregano and chilli flakes and a drizzle of olive oil, before serving.

Serves 4–6

1–1.3kg/2¼–3lb beef flank

about 475ml/16fl oz/2 cups tomato sauce (see page 26)

3 balls mozzarella cheese, thinly sliced

15ml/1 tbsp dried oregano

5ml/1 tsp dried chilli flakes

salt and ground black pepper

30ml/2 tbsp olive oil, for drizzling

Energy 393kcal/1637kJ; Protein 39g; Carbohydrate 4g, of which sugars 4g; Fat 24g, of which saturates 8g; Cholesterol 97mg; Calcium 24mg; Fibre 1g; Sodium 145mg.

Stuffed beef flank
Matambre

Matambre means 'hunger killer', and this is a great dish when entertaining as it looks impressive and can be prepared well in advance. It is made with beef flank, bashed until flat enough to stuff and roll, and can be served hot or cold, accompanied by salad and chimichurri sauce or mayonnaise.

Serves 4

1kg/2¼lb beef flank

a few sprigs of thyme

2 medium carrots, coarsely grated

250g/9oz fresh spinach, steamed and well-drained

10 eggs, hard-boiled for 7 minutes, peeled

25g/1oz/2 sachets powdered gelatine

30ml/2 tbsp olive oil

about 3 litres/5 pints/12½ cups beef stock

salt and ground black pepper

chimichurri, to serve

Cook's Tip Use matambre and chimichurri leftovers the next day for a delicious sandwich filling.

1 Trim the beef, then 'butterfly' it by slicing through it lengthwise, almost to the other side, and opening it like a book. Put the meat between two sheets of clear film (plastic wrap), outside facing down, and gently bash all over with a meat mallet or rolling pin until it is an even thickness. Season the meat, then sprinkle over the thyme leaves.

2 Scatter the grated carrots over the seasoned meat, leaving a border of about 2.5cm/1in at the top and bottom. Arrange the spinach leaves on top of the carrots.

3 Slice off the top and bases, of the peeled hard-boiled eggs, so they are flat at both ends and you can almost see the yolk (this will help when rolling and when sliced you will have egg yolk in every slice). Arrange them, so that the flat ends join together in a line along the edge of the meat nearest to you.

4 With your fingertips, sprinkle the gelatine evenly all over the filling and season again with a little salt and pepper.

5 Roll the meat up into a cylinder, like a Swiss roll (jelly roll), as tightly as possible, starting from the end with the eggs, then using butcher's string, tightly tie in several places, starting in the middle, then about 2cm/¾in from the ends, then further ties as necessary, about 3cm/1¼in apart.

6 Heat the oil in a large casserole, and when hot, add the beef. Sear on all sides, turning, for about 5 minutes. Pour over just enough of the stock to cover the beef, place a weight on top and bring to the boil. Cover and simmer gently for 2–2½ hours or until the meat is very tender, turning over halfway through cooking.

7 Transfer the matambre to a board and let it rest for 15 minutes. Remove the string and cut crossways into 2.5cm/1in slices. Spoon over some of the cooking juices and serve hot.

8 Alternatively, place another board on top of the matambre and top with a weight. When cool, chill in the refrigerator for at least 2 hours before slicing and serving cold.

Energy 743kcal/3094kJ; Protein 80g; Carbohydrate 5g, of which sugars 5g; Fat 45g, of which saturates 15g; Cholesterol 625mg; Calcium 219mg; Fibre 4g; Sodium 710mg.

Stuffed beef escalopes
Niños envuelto

Litterally translated niños envuelto means 'wrapped-up children'. These rolls contain a tasty filling of bacon, cheese and grilled peppers. They are braised in white wine and stock, which can be thickened with a little cornflour to make a sauce.

1 Preheat the oven to 180°C/350°F/Gas 4. Place the beef between sheets of clear film (plastic wrap), and gently pound with a meat mallet or rolling pin until very thin.

2 Season with salt and pepper, then thinly spread with mustard. Place a rasher of bacon on each escalope, top with a slice of cheese, half a pepper, and two basil leaves.

3 Roll up each piece of beef and use kitchen string to secure the seam and the ends. Place in an ovenproof dish and pour over the wine and stock. Cover with a lid or foil and bake for 20 minutes or until the beef is tender.

4 Remove the string and serve the beef with a little of the cooking juices poured over, mashed potatoes and steamed green vegetables such as spring greens or green beans.

Cook's Tip To prepare your own peppers, cut two red (bell) peppers into quarters, discarding the seeds. In a bowl, toss the peppers with 15ml/1 tbsp olive oil and a little salt and pepper. Place, skin side up on a foil-lined grill (broiler) pan under a hot grill for 4–5 minutes or until the skins are blistered and blackened. Turn and cook for a further minute or until tender. Put the peppers in a plastic bag and leave to cool, then peel off the charred skins.

Serves 4

4 beef escalopes, each weighing about 150g/5oz

30ml/2 tbsp mild mustard

4 rashers (strips) of smoked back bacon, trimmed

4 slices of Cheddar cheese

2 bottled or grilled (bell) peppers (see Cook's Tip), seeded and halved

8 basil leaves

150ml/¼ pint/⅔ cup white wine

150ml/¼ pint/⅔ cup beef stock

salt and ground black pepper

Energy 370kcal/1545kJ; Protein 42g; Carbohydrate 3g, of which sugars 3g; Fat 21g, of which saturates 10g; Cholesterol 124mg; Calcium 167mg; Fibre 2g; Sodium 862mg.

Creole beef and pumpkin stew
Carbonada criolla

Serves 4

45ml/3 tbsp olive oil

3 onions, chopped

1 red (bell) pepper, chopped

4 cloves garlic, chopped

500g/1¼lb lean braising steak, cut into 5cm/2in cubes

5ml/1 tsp ground paprika

5ml/1 tsp dried oregano

5ml/1 tsp dried chilli flakes

15ml/1 tbsp soft brown sugar

2 tomatoes, chopped

475ml/16fl oz/2 cups beef stock

2 medium carrots, diced

3 medium potatoes, cut into 2.5cm/1in cubes

500g/1¼lb pumpkin, cut into 2.5cm/1in cubes

4 whole corn cobs

3 fresh peaches, peeled and cut into wedges or 8 ready-to-eat dried apricots, halved

115g/4oz/scant 1 cup raisins

salt and ground black pepper

Originally this would have been slowly simmered over the hot embers of an open fire until all that was left was ashes (carbonada). The dish was adopted by the 'criollos', Spanish descendants born in the country during colonial times.

1 Heat half of the oil in a large pan and cook the onions for 3–4 minutes, stirring. Add the pepper and garlic and cook for 2–3 minutes more. Remove from the pan and set aside.

2 Heat the remaining oil in the pan and cook the beef until well-browned. Return the onion mixture to the pan with the paprika, oregano, chilli flakes and sugar. Cook for 2 minutes, then stir in the tomatoes and stock. Season, bring to the boil, cover and simmer for 30 minutes.

3 Stir in the carrots, potatoes and pumpkin, re-cover the pan and cook for 15–20 minutes.

4 Use a sharp knife to cut away the kernels from the corn and add them to the pan with the peaches or apricots and raisins. Simmer for a further 5 minutes. Leave to stand for a few minutes before serving.

Cook's Tip To serve in a whole pumpkin, cut the top off a large pumpkin and scoop out the seeds. Make a few holes inside with a fork (but don't pierce the skin) Sprinkle 30ml/2 tbsp sugar inside and add 250ml/8fl oz/1 cup milk. Bake in an oven at 160°C/325°F/Gas 3 for 1 hour or until just tender. Tip away any liquid, then fill with stew and serve.

Energy 714kcal/3005kJ; Protein 40g; Carbohydrate 93g, of which sugars 50g; Fat 23g, of which saturates 5g; Cholesterol 79mg; Calcium 125mg; Fibre 16g; Sodium 318mg.

Beef stew
Puchero

Serves 4–6

500g/1¼lb braising beef

4 beef marrow bones

2 bay leaves

a few sprigs of thyme

2 onions, quartered

2 small leeks, sliced

2 sticks celery, thickly sliced

2 small carrots, quartered

225g/8oz/1¼ cups dried
butter (lima) beans, soaked
overnight and drained

2 corn cobs, cut into 3 chunks

2 large potatoes, quartered

½ butternut squash, cut into
chunks

225g/8oz pancetta, diced

4 pork sausages

salt and ground black pepper

bread and olive oil, for serving

This classic dish comes from the Pampas region of Argentina. It relies on the use of a variety of meats and vegetables and never includes strongly flavoured spices. A cross between a soup and a stew, the liquid should be a thin broth, not thick gravy.

1 Dice the beef into 7.5cm/3in pieces and place in a large pan, together with the bones. Add the bay leaves, thyme and a little salt, then add 3 litres/5 pints/12 cups water. Bring to the boil and skim. Add the onions, leeks, celery and carrots and bring back to the boil.

2 Cover the pan and simmer for 1¼ hours, then remove the bones and discard. Drain the butter beans and add to the pan.

3 Cover the pan and cook for 15 minutes more. Add the corn pieces, potato, squash, diced pancetta and sausages. Simmer, covered, for a further 30 minutes or until the meat and vegetables are tender.

4 Season to taste with salt and pepper and ladle the stew into warmed pasta plates or large bowls, sharing the meat equally. Drizzle with a little olive oil, and serve with bread.

Energy 308kcal/1296kJ; Protein 29g; Carbohydrate 30g, of which sugars 8g; Fat 9g, of which saturates 3g; Cholesterol 60mg; Calcium 95mg; Fibre 10g; Sodium 226mg.

Argentinian-style barbecue

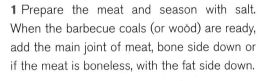
Asado

Lunchtime asados are an important part of Argentinian life, eaten at home or at a restaurant specializing in grilled fare. The tradition is to supply more than enough; it is a hosting disaster to be short of something. Chorizo, morcilla and sweetbread is always included, together with some meat on the bone.

1 Prepare the meat and season with salt. When the barbecue coals (or wood) are ready, add the main joint of meat, bone side down or if the meat is boneless, with the fat side down.

2 When the meat has begun to sizzle, add the chicken, kidneys, intestines, chorizo and sweetbreads, then the skirt and flank. When each piece is half-cooked, turn it over – do this only once, don't prod or pierce the meat or you will release juices. Don't move the meat around once it has started cooking; if it needs more heat, move hot coals beneath it. Season with a little salt and pepper during cooking, if liked.

3 About 20 minutes before the meat is ready, add the black pudding and provoleta cheese (see page 45). Serve with salads, breads and sauces such as chimichurri. If you wish, serve the chorizos with chimichurri in mini baguettes, briefly toasted on the barbecue.

Cook's tip Asado is always served in three courses, so remove from the grill and serve in this order:
1 black pudding, chorizo and provoleta
2 sweetbreads, chitterlings, kidneys, slisces of skirt and flank
3 main meat, cut into pieces or sliced.

Serves 4

500g/1¼lb costillar (beef short rib) per person, or 500g/ 1¼lb lechon (suckling pig) per person, or 500g/1¼lb cordero (lamb) per person

a chicken, 2kg/4½lb in weight, spatchcocked

2 kidneys, halved and trimmed

1kg/2¼lb chinchulines (chitterlings/beef intestines)

4 chorizo (pork sausages)

1kg/2¼lb mollejas (sweetbreads)

1 entrana (piece of beef skirt) or 1 matambre (beef flank)

2 morcillas (black pudding)

4 provoleta (provolone cheese)

salt (preferably sea salt flakes) and ground black pepper

salads, bread and sauces such as chimichurri, to serve

Energy 2637kcal/10988kJ; Protein 199g; Carbohydrate 20g, of which sugars 1g; Fat 195g, of which saturates 85g; Cholesterol 1202mg; Calcium 1196mg; Fibre 0g; Sodium 2822mg.

Ox tongue with vinaigrette sauce
Lengua a la vinagreta

Argentinians make good use of all cuts of meat and offal and little is wasted. Meats prepared in 'escabeche' (marinating after or instead of cooking in an acidic marinade – usually lemon juice or vinegar) or served with a vinaigrette are common in South American cooking as it was a way of keeping meat for longer during hot weather before refrigeration. This dish is often an accompaniment to an asado (barbecue).

1 Place the ox tongue in a large pan with the onion, leek, carrots, bay leaves, clove, thyme and clove of garlic. Pour over just enough cold water to cover.

2 Slowly bring to the boil, skim off any surface scum, then reduce the heat so that the water simmers steadily. Cover and simmer for 2 hours, or until the meat is tender when pierced with a small knife. Leave the tongue to cool in its cooking liquid until it is just cool enough for you to handle.

3 Drain the tongue and discard the cooking liquid. Cut away any tough white gristle at the wide end of the tongue, if necessary (this may have already been removed by the butcher). Peel off the thick skin, and cut the tongue into slices no thicker than 2cm/³⁄₄in.

4 For the vinaigrette, whisk together the vinegar and oil in a jug (pitcher), then stir in the peppers, garlic, onion and parsley. Season to taste with salt and pepper.

5 Arrange the tongue slices on a large serving dish, one at a time, spooning a little vinaigrette over each slice, as you go. Cover with clear film (plastic wrap) and chill in the refrigerator for at least 2 hours, but preferably overnight, to allow the meat to soak up the flavours. Serve with grated hard-boiled eggs and chopped parsley.

Serves 4–6

1 small ox tongue

1 Spanish (Bermuda) onion, peeled and quartered

1 small leek, sliced

2 small carrots, sliced

2 bay leaves

1 clove

a few sprigs of thyme

1 clove garlic, peeled

For the vinaigrette

60ml/4 tbsp red wine vinegar

100ml/3¹⁄₂fl oz/scant ¹⁄₂ cup olive oil

1 red (bell) pepper, seeded and diced

1 green (bell) pepper, seeded and diced

1 yellow (bell) pepper, seeded and diced

4 garlic cloves, finely chopped

1 Spanish (Bermuda) or red onion, finely chopped

salt and ground black pepper

2 hard-boiled eggs, shelled and grated, and chopped fresh parsley, to serve

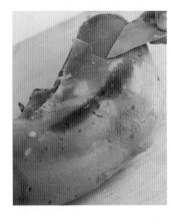

Energy 489kcal/2031kJ; Protein 26g; Carbohydrate 6g, of which sugars 5g; Fat 40g, of which saturates 3g; Cholesterol 64mg; Calcium 33mg; Fibre 2g; Sodium 1031mg.

Rose veal with tuna sauce

Vitel toné

Christmas and New Year would not be the same in Argentina without this dish, which originated in the Lombardy and Piedmont regions of northern Italy in the 19th century (where it is known as vittelo tonatto). Usually served as a cold appetizer, it consists of slices of veal in a tuna sauce, and is perfect for serving in the heat of the festive season in the southern hemisphere.

Serves 4–8

1kg/2¼lb piece boneless rose veal topside

1 small carrot, halved

1 large onion, quartered

2 celery sticks, halved

2 bay leaves

a few sprigs of thyme

For the tuna sauce

12 salted anchovies

2 cloves garlic, peeled

30ml/2 tbsp capers, drained, plus 5ml/1 tsp, to garnish

10ml/2 tsp Dijon mustard

5ml/1 tsp lemon juice

250g/9oz canned tuna

250ml/8fl oz/1 cup mayonnaise

100ml/3½fl oz/scant ½ cup double (heavy) cream

salt and ground black pepper

4 hard-boiled eggs, grated, chopped chives, and capers, to garnish

olive oil, to drizzle

green salad and bread, to serve

Cook's Tip Rose veal is pale pink before it is cooked, and is reared in welfare friendly conditions, unlike milk-fed veal, which is from younger calves. If it is unavailable, leftover turkey breast can be used.

1 Put the veal in a pan with the carrot, onion, celery, bay leaves, thyme and a pinch of salt.

2 Pour over enough cold water to cover, then bring to the boil. Reduce the heat, cover the pan and simmer for 1–1½ hours.

3 When the veal is cooked and tender. Lift the joint out of the stock and leave to cool, then chill for at least 2 hours.

4 Meanwhile, make the sauce. Put the anchovies, garlic, capers, mustard, lemon juice and tuna in a food processor. Blend to a smooth paste.

5 Spoon and scrape the tuna mixture into a bowl and whisk in the mayonnaise and cream. Cover and chill until needed.

6 When the veal is cool, carve across the grain, into slices no thicker than 2cm/¾in and arrange on a large serving platter or on individual plates.

7 Spoon the tuna sauce over the meat and scatter over the grated hard-boiled eggs, some chopped chives and 5ml/1 tsp capers. Drizzle with olive oil and add plenty of freshly ground black pepper. Serve with a green salad and some fresh bread.

Energy 483kcal/2010kJ; Protein 39g; Carbohydrate 1g, of which sugars 1g; Fat 36g, of which saturates 9g; Cholesterol 217mg; Calcium 45mg; Fibre 1g; Sodium 546mg.

Roast lamb
Cordero asado

Although beef is Argentina's favourite meat, lamb is also enjoyed, especially in Patagonia where there are more sheep than cattle. Patagonian lamb is highly regarded in export markets as its quality is superb, with a lower fat content largely due to the vast ranges of natural grassland it feeds on.

1 Preheat the oven to 160°C/325°F/Gas 3. Peel 12 cloves of the garlic. Make 12 small incisions all over the skin of the lamb. Rub the lamb with olive oil and season well with salt and pepper, then insert a clove of garlic and a tiny sprig of rosemary into each slit.

2 Heat a large frying pan over a high heat and add 45ml/3 tbsp olive oil. Sear the lamb in the pan, turning until it is browned all over (take care not to displace the garlic and rosemary). Place the lamb in a roasting pan and roast in the oven for 30 minutes.

3 Add the remaining unpeeled garlic cloves to the roasting pan with the rest of the rosemary. Pour over the wine and stock and cook for a further 1–1¼ hours, depending on how well you like it cooked, basting occasionally.

4 Remove the lamb from the oven and transfer to a board. Cover with foil and leave to rest for 15–20 minutes. Transfer the juices from the roasting pan into a small pan. Skim off the fat, then boil the juices rapidly for a few minutes, until well-reduced, thick and syrupy.

5 Towards the end of cooking, cut the potatoes into chunks and cook in boiling salted water for 15 minutes or until tender. Drain well, then return to the pan and mash. Add the butter, cream and milk and beat well with a wooden spoon. Add the mustard, beat again and season to taste with salt and pepper.

6 Carve the lamb and serve with the roasted garlic cloves and mashed potatoes, with sauce spooned over the top.

Serves 4–6

small leg of lamb, about 2kg/4½lb

3 bulbs of garlic

olive oil

1 bunch of rosemary

250ml/8fl oz/1 cup white wine

350ml/12fl oz/1½ cups lamb or beef stock

1kg/2¼lb potatoes, such as maris piper or king Edwards, peeled

50g/2oz/4 tbsp butter

100ml/3½fl oz/scant ½ cup double (heavy) cream

45ml/3 tbsp milk

45ml/3 tbsp wholegrain mustard

salt and ground black pepper

steamed purple sprouting broccoli or sautéed turnip tops, to serve

Energy 585kcal/2439kJ; Protein 39g; Carbohydrate 30g, of which sugars 2g; Fat 35g, of which saturates 17g; Cholesterol 164mg; Calcium 57mg; Fibre 3g; Sodium 404mg.

Stuffed lamb breast
Pechito de cordero relleno

This is another recipe from the Patagonia region, where lamb and goat are very popular. The land and climate are perfect for grazing, and lamb from this region is very tender. One of the least expensive cuts of lamb, breast is full of flavour but needs to be cooked slowly.

Serves 4–6

2 handfuls dried morel mushrooms

1 handful sun-dried tomatoes

2 cloves garlic, peeled

1 large onion, quartered

4 sprigs of rosemary leaves

1 egg white

45ml/3 tbsp double (heavy) cream

150ml/¼ pint/⅔ cup port

2 lamb breasts, boned and ready to roll

salt and ground black pepper

30ml/2 tbsp olive oil

475ml/16fl oz/2 cups stock

roasted sweet potatoes and green beans, to serve

Cook's Tip Breast may not be on display at the butchers but should be available. Ask for the meat to be boned, skinned and rolled, and ask for extra string for rerolling once stuffed.

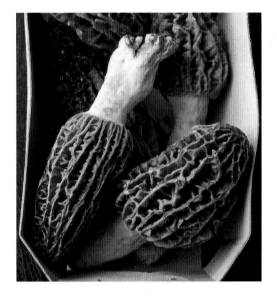

1 Soak the dried mushrooms and sun-dried tomatoes in separate bowls in warm water for 1 hour, changing the water several times. Drain well, then squeeze out the soaking liquid and set the mushrooms and tomatoes aside.

2 Put the garlic, onion, rosemary leaves and half the mushrooms in a food processor and blend to a paste. Spoon and scrape the mixture into a bowl.

3 Lightly whisk the egg white until frothy, then add to the mushroom mixture, add the cream and 60ml/4 tbsp of the port. Mix well and season to taste with salt and pepper.

4 Place the lamb breasts on a chopping board, skin side down and spread half the mushroom purée mixture on each breast. Sprinkle the rest of the mushrooms and dried tomatoes evenly over the lamb, then roll up the lamb and tie each with butcher's string in four or five places.

5 Preheat the oven to 180°C/350°F/Gas 4. Heat the oil in a large frying pan and sear the lamb, one at a time, on all sides until browned. Transfer the lamb to a roasting pan and pour over the remaining port and stock. Cover with foil and cook in the oven for 45 minutes.

6 Lift the lamb out of the roasting pan and leave to rest, covered, for 15 minutes. Skim the fat from the meat juices, then transfer the juices into a pan and boil for a few minutes to reduce. Carve the meat into thick slices and serve with the juices, and with roasted sweet potatoes and green beans.

Energy 586kcal/2433kJ; Protein 38g; Carbohydrate 5g, of which sugars 4g; Fat 46g, of which saturates 21g; Cholesterol 160mg; Calcium 39mg; Fibre 4g; Sodium 368mg.

Stout-braised pork tenderloin
Solomillo de cerdo a la cerveza negra

Argentina is renowned for its wine production, and less well-known for its beer. Some excellent ones are made in the country, however, especially in the south where German communities settled.

1 Preheat the oven to 160°C/325°F/Gas 3. Season the tenderloins with salt and pepper. Heat the oil in a large frying pan and fry the meat over a high heat until lightly browned on all sides. Transfer to a casserole dish.

2 Add the vegetables to the frying pan and cook for 4–5 minutes, stirring frequently over a high heat until beginning to colour. Add to the pork with the rosemary and thyme. Pour the beer into the frying pan, bring to the boil and boil rapidly until reduced by about half.

3 Add the reduced beer into the casserole dish with the pork and vegtables, and add enough stock to cover. Place the lid on the casserole and cook in the oven for 1½–2 hours.

4 While the pork is cooking, remove the centres of each apple with an apple corer. Cut a sliver off the base, so that they will stand upright and score around their circumference with a sharp knife. Place in a small baking dish. Mix the sugar and butter together and divide between the apple cavities. Add 30ml/2 tbsp water to the dish, cover with foil and bake for 45 minutes.

5 Lift out the meat with a slotted spoon and set aside. Bring the cooking juices to a rapid boil and reduce by about half. Strain the sauce through a fine sieve into a clean pan, discarding the vegetables and herbs.

6 Carve the meat into thick medallions and gently re-heat in the sauce if necessary. Serve the pork with the sauce spooned over, together with the baked apples, creamed potatoes, and steamed curly kale.

Serves 4

2 pork tenderloins, halved

30ml/2 tbsp olive oil

4 garlic cloves

1 Spanish (Bermuda) onion, quartered

1 carrot, cut into 4 pieces

1 leek, cut into 4 pieces

2 celery sticks, each cut into 4 pieces

2 sprigs of rosemary

2 sprigs of thyme

1 bay leaf

600ml/1 pint/2½ cups stout such as Guinness

about 1 litre/1¾ pints/4 cups beef stock

salt and ground black pepper

creamed potatoes and steamed curly kale, to serve

For the baked apples

4 eating apples

30ml/2 tbsp soft light brown sugar

15ml/1 tbsp butter

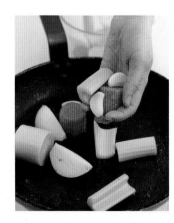

Energy 515kcal/2154kJ; Protein 47g; Carbohydrate 30g, of which sugars 28g; Fat 24g, of which saturates 8g; Cholesterol 134mg; Calcium 58mg; Fibre 6g; Sodium 407mg.

Chorizo hot pot
Chorizo a la pomarola

This quick and easy dish is often eaten in rural areas where it is sometimes cooked in a pot made from a used 'disco de arado'; the iron disc from a tractor plough. After welding sides onto the disc, the pot may be used for cooking over charcoal.

1 Heat the olive oil in a frying pan and fry the sausages for a few minutes over a medium heat until beginning to colour on each side.

2 Add the onions, garlic and peppers to the pan. Turn down the heat and continue cooking for 4–5 minutes, until beginning to soften.

3 Add the tomato purée and cook for a minute or two, stirring, then pour in the wine and simmer for a minute. Add the chopped tomatoes, bay leaf, thyme, oregano, paprika and salt and pepper to taste. Cover with a lid and cook for 20–25 minutes. Serve with mashed potatoes or bread.

Serves 4

30ml/2 tbsp olive oil

8 Argentinian chorizo or good quality pork sausages

2 large onions, sliced

2 cloves garlic, chopped

1 red (bell) pepper, seeded and sliced

1 green (bell) pepper, seeded and sliced

15ml/1 tbsp tomato purée (paste)

250ml/8fl oz/1 cup white wine

3 beefsteak tomatoes, chopped

1 bay leaf

a few sprigs of thyme

15ml/1 tbsp dried oregano

15ml/1 tbsp ground paprika

salt and ground black pepper

mashed potatoes or bread, to serve

Energy 465kcal/1932kJ; Protein 23g; Carbohydrate 18g, of which sugars 15g; Fat 34g, of which saturates 12g; Cholesterol 79mg; Calcium 34mg; Fibre 4g; Sodium 668mg.

Calf's liver and onion
Higado con cebollas

Serves 4

4 slices calf's liver, each weighing about 150g/5oz

flour, for dusting

45ml/3 tbsp olive oil

25g/1oz/2 tbsp butter

3 red onions, thinly sliced

2 garlic cloves, finely chopped

few sprigs of thyme

250ml/8fl oz/1 cup port

475ml/16fl oz/2 cups beef stock

salt and ground black pepper

mashed potatoes and a green vegetable, to serve

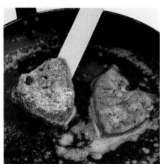

In Argentina calf's liver is cheap and widely available. Be careful not to overcook the liver or it will toughen; it should be still be pink in the middle.

1 Rinse the liver in cold water and pat it dry on kitchen paper. Season the flour, put it on a plate and coat the liver in it.

2 Heat the oil and butter in a frying pan, add the liver and cook for about 1 minute, then turn over and cook the other side for a further minute, until lightly browned and just firm. Remove and keep warm.

3 Add the onions and garlic to the pan and fry for 7–8 minutes or until soft. Add the thyme, then pour in the port and cook over a high heat until well-reduced. Add the stock and reduce again to about half its original volume. Remove the thyme and discard. Serve the liver with the sauce spooned over.

Cook's Tip Crispy pancetta and fried onions are a classic accompaniment to this dish. For crispy pancetta, line a baking tray with baking parchment and arrange slices of pancetta in a single layer. Place a second sheet of baking parchment on top, then cover with another baking tray to prevent it curling. Cook at 160°C/325°F/Gas 3 for 20–25 minutes.

For fried onions, melt 50g/2oz/½ cup of butter in a large pan. Add two thinly sliced onions and mix to coat with butter. Cover and cook on a low heat for 10 minutes, stirring occasionally. Stir in 5ml/1 tsp sugar, re-cover the pan and cook for a further 10 minutes, or until they are soft and golden. Increase the heat, remove the lid and stir the onions over a high heat until they are crisp and golden.

Energy 367kcal/1528kJ; Protein 30g; Carbohydrate 13g, of which sugars 6g; Fat 22g, of which saturates 6g; Cholesterol 568mg; Calcium 46mg; Fibre 2g; Sodium 442mg.

Tripe stew
Buseca

Much-loved by Argentinians, tripe should be gently cooked until meltingly tender. Unlike some European recipes where it is cooked in a creamy white sauce, buseca is a vibrant well-flavoured dish with a combination of tomatoes, peppers, beans, red wine and pungent herbs. Buseca is traditionally enjoyed with a glass of red wine.

1 Thoroughly rinse the tripe under cold running water, then put in a bowl with plenty of cold water to cover. Add the vinegar and leave to soak for at least 30 minutes.

2 Rinse the tripe again, then put in a pan and cover with cold water. Slowly bring to the boil, lower the heat and cover the pan with a lid. Gently simmer for about 2 hours, or until tender. Drain the tripe and leave to cool, then cut into bitesize pieces with kitchen scissors.

3 Heat the oil in the rinsed out pan and add the pancetta and chorizo. Cook over a low heat for 3–4 minutes, then add the onion, pepper, carrot and leek. Cook for 5 minutes, or until beginning to soften. Add the garlic, thyme, bay leaf and paprika. Stir for a minute or two, then pour in the red wine.

4 Simmer uncovered for a few minutes, then add the chopped tomatoes and cabbage. Return the tripe to the pan and season with salt and pepper. Cover with the lid and cook for 10 minutes over a low heat.

5 Stir in the butter beans and chickpeas. Cover the pan and cook for a further 5–10 minutes or until the vegetables are tender. Serve with bread and glasses of red wine.

Cook's Tip Check with your butcher when buying tripe; it is usually sold cleaned, washed and blanched, but may be fully cooked, in which case you needn't clean and cook the tripe as in steps 1 and 2.

Serves 4

500g/1¼lb tripe

45ml/3 tbsp white wine vinegar

30ml/2 tbsp olive oil

100g/3¾oz pancetta, diced

100g/3¾oz Spanish chorizo, diced

1 large onion, chopped

1 red (bell) pepper) seeded and chopped

1 large carrot, cut into small dice

1 leek, cut into small dice

2 garlic cloves, chopped

a few sprigs of fresh thyme

1 bay leaf

15ml/1 tbsp paprika

250ml/8fl oz/1 cup red wine

400g/14oz can tomatoes

100g/4oz white cabbage, very thinly sliced

200g/7oz can butter (lima) beans, drained and rinsed

200g/7oz can chickpeas, drained and rinsed

salt and ground black pepper

bread and red wine, to serve

Energy 391kcal/1636kJ; Protein 27g; Carbohydrate 24g, of which sugars 10g; Fat 21g, of which saturates 6g; Cholesterol 99mg; Calcium 141mg; Fibre 7g; Sodium 730mg.

Tripe and corn stew with hot chilli sauce
Locro

One of the national dishes of Argentina, locro is a thick and hearty stew that originates from the Andes. It is often served on May 25th, 'May Revolution' day. Quiquirimichi, a flavoured oil made from onions, dried red chilli peppers and paprika, is the traditional accompaniment to locro.

Serves 4–6

45ml/3 tbsp vegetable oil

100g/3¾oz pancetta, diced

1 Spanish chorizo, diced

150g/5oz braising steak, diced

2 pig's trotters (feet), each cut into 4 pieces

3 pork sausages or Argentinian chorizo, halved

300g/11oz/1½ cups dried white corn, soaked in cold water overnight

100g/3¾oz/½ cup dried butter (lima) beans, soaked in cold water overnight

5ml/1 tsp ground cumin

15ml/1 tbsp paprika

2 medium leeks, cut into small dice

200g/7oz pumpkin, diced

250ml/8fl oz/1 cup vegetable stock

200g/7oz tripe, cooked and diced (see page 94)

salt and ground black pepper

bread, to serve

For the quiquirimichi

75ml/5 tbsp vegetable oil

1 bunch of spring onions (scallions), sliced

5ml/1 tsp paprika

15ml/1 tbsp dried chilli flakes

1 Heat the oil in a large pan. Add the pancetta and Spanish chorizo and cook for 4–5 minutes until beginning to colour. Add the beef and stir for 2–3 minutes until brown. Add the pig's trotters and sausages. Cook over a medium heat for 10 minutes, stirring often.

2 Drain the corn and butter beans and add to the pan, followed by the cumin and paprika. Cook for a few minutes, then add the leeks and pumpkin and continue cooking for 5 minutes.

3 Pour in the stock and season with salt and pepper, to taste. Bring to the boil, then lower the heat to a gentle simmer, cover and cook for 30 minutes, stirring occasionally.

4 Add the tripe to the pan and cook for a further 45 minutes to 1 hour, stirring from time to time. Add a little more stock or water, if needed, to prevent it drying out. When the pumpkin is beginning to fall apart and the corn and butter beans are very tender, the locro is ready, the consistency should be like a thick creamy soup.

5 Meanwhile, make the quiquirimichi. Pour the oil into a small pan and put over a low heat. Add the spring onions and spices and cook for 10 minutes, stirring frequently. Turn off the heat and leave to cool for 15 minutes, then add 15ml/1 tbsp cold water. Leave to stand, so that the oil floats to the top.

6 Ladle the locro into warmed bowls. Scoop the oil from the top of the quiquirimichi and drizzle on top of the locro. Serve with bread.

Energy 544kcal/2262kJ; Protein 28g; Carbohydrate 16g, of which sugars 5g; Fat 41g, of which saturates 10g; Cholesterol 95mg; Calcium 120mg; Fibre 5g; Sodium 767mg.

Sautéed kidneys with garlic
Riñones al ajillo

Serves 4–6

1kg/2¼lb calf's or lamb's kidneys

60ml/4 tbsp white wine vinegar

30ml/2 tbsp olive oil

2 Spanish (Bermuda) onions, finely chopped

6 garlic cloves, chopped

120ml/4fl oz/½ cup white wine

15g/½oz/1 tbsp butter

½ small bunch of parsley, finely chopped

salt and ground black pepper

toasted bread, to serve

Kidneys have a deliciously rich flavour, here enhanced by garlic and white wine. When spit-roasting a whole lamb, it is usually the asador's perk (the person in charge of barbecue cooking) to eat the kidneys as a reward for all his hard work.

1 Cut the kidneys in half. Using kitchen scissors, snip out the tubes and pale core. Put the kidneys in a bowl of cold water and add the vinegar. Leave to soak for 30 minutes. Drain the kidneys and pat dry on kitchen paper, then cut into 2cm/¾in thick slices.

2 Heat the oil in a large frying pan. Add the kidneys and cook, stirring constantly, over a high heat for 2–3 minutes. Turn down the heat to medium, add the onions and cook for 5 minutes until soft.

3 Add the garlic to the pan and cook for a further 2–3 minutes. Season with salt and pepper. Pour in the wine and simmer until the liquid has reduced to about a third.

4 Turn the heat to very low and stir in the butter to give the sauce body and shine.

5 Remove from the heat and stir in most of the parsley. Leave to stand for a minute, then serve on warmed plates, sprinkle with the remaining parsley and serve with toasted bread.

Energy 240kcal/1006kJ; Protein 29g; Carbohydrate 5g, of which sugars 3g; Fat 12g, of which saturates 4g; Cholesterol 530mg; Calcium 37mg; Fibre 1g; Sodium 269mg.

Sweetbreads in white wine sauce

Mollejas al vino blanco

Sweetbreads are a delicacy in Argentina and served in numerous ways, including pan-frying, and braising. They are often cooked as one of the courses at an asado, but when not barbecuing, this quick and simple recipe is a popular alternative.

1 Soak the sweetbreads in cold water for 2 hours, changing the water several times. Rinse well. Put in a pan with the onion, garlic cloves, bay leaf, thyme and lemon juice. Pour over cold water to cover and bring to the boil. Reduce the heat and simmer for 5 minutes, until the sweetbreads are firm and white.

2 Drain the sweetbreads and plunge into a bowl of iced water to stop further cooking. Drain again, then peel off the membrane and remove any pieces of gristle or fat. Cut into slices about 2cm/³⁄₄in thick. Season the slices with salt and pepper and lightly dust in flour.

3 Heat the oil and butter in a large frying pan over a high heat. Cook the sweetbreads (in batches), for 1–2 minutes on each side. Remove from the pan and keep warm.

4 Add the spring onions and garlic to the pan and cook for 2 minutes, stirring. Pour in the wine, increase the heat and boil until the liquid is reduced to about a third of its volume.

5 Divide the sweetbreads between warmed plates and spoon over the sauce. Garnish with lemon wedges and serve with sliced sautéed or steamed potatoes.

Serves 4–6

1kg/2¼lb sweetbreads (preferably veal)

1 onion, quartered

2 garlic cloves, peeled

1 bay leaf

a few sprigs of fresh thyme

juice of 1 lemon

plain (all-purpose) flour, for dusting

30ml/2 tbsp olive oil

15g/½oz/1 tbsp butter

1 bunch of spring onions (scallions), sliced

2 cloves garlic, finely chopped

250ml/8fl oz/1 cup white wine

salt and ground black pepper

lemon wedges, to garnish

sautéed or steamed potatoes, to serve

Energy 312kcal/1304kJ; Protein 26g; Carbohydrate 7g, of which sugars 3g; Fat 20g, of which saturates 7g; Cholesterol 439mg; Calcium 54mg; Fibre 1g; Sodium 144mg.

Rabbit 'al disco'
Conejo al disco de arado

This rabbit dish is cooked 'Al disco de arado' on the huge iron disc salvaged from a plough, and is cooked over a wood fire. A large cast-iron frying pan makes a good substitute. Rabbit is, of course, a staple rural ingredient, and this recipe makes the most of its flavour in a lovely herby casserole.

Serves 4

4 large or 8 small rabbit portions

salt and ground black pepper

45ml/3 tbsp olive oil

2 large onions, finely chopped

3 medium carrots, diced

2 green (bell) peppers, diced

1 medium leek, diced

4 garlic cloves, crushed

15ml/1 tbsp paprika

120ml/4fl oz/1/2 cup white wine

120ml/4fl oz/1/2 cup chicken stock

200g/7oz can chopped tomatoes

2 bay leaves

a few sprigs of thyme

5ml/1 tsp dried oregano

2.5ml/1/2 tsp dried tarragon

200g/7oz frozen peas

steamed or pilau rice, to serve

1 Season the rabbit with salt and pepper. Heat the oil in a large frying pan, add the rabbit and fry the meat over a high heat for 2–3 minutes on each side until dark golden. Remove from the pan and set aside.

2 Lower the heat to medium and add the onions, cook, stirring, for 2–3 minutes.

3 Add the diced carrots, peppers and leek to the onions, and cook for a further 3–4 minutes, still stirring, then add the crushed garlic and paprika and cook for 2–3 minutes more, stirring all the time.

4 Return the rabbit pieces to the pan, pour over the wine and bring to the boil, then simmer, uncovered until the wine has reduced by half.

5 Turn down the heat to low and add the stock, chopped tomatoes, bay leaves, thyme, oregano and tarragon. Cover with a lid and simmer for 45 minutes to 1 hour or until the rabbit is cooked through and tender.

6 While the rabbit is cooking, spread the peas out on a plate and leave to defrost at room temperature. Add to the pan 5 minutes before the end of cooking time. Check the seasoning and add more salt and pepper if needed.

7 Serve the rabbit piled on warmed plates with the vegetables and sauce. Accompany with steamed or pilau rice.

Energy 475kcal/1988kJ; Protein 47g; Carbohydrate 21g, of which sugars 14g; Fat 23g, of which saturates 6g; Cholesterol 99mg; Calcium 117mg; Fibre 9g; Sodium 211mg.

Venison loin with cherries
Lomo de ciervo con cerezas

Venison is a dark, close-textured meat with very little fat. Tender prime cuts such as loin are usually served rare or medium. Here, dark cherries cooked with red wine and a dash of vinegar provide an excellent contrast for the rich meat.

1 Preheat the oven to 180°C/350°F/Gas 4. Pat the venison dry with kitchen paper and season with salt and pepper. Heat the oil in a heavy frying pan, add the meat and fry for 2–3 minutes over a high heat, on each side until browned.

2 Turn down the heat and add the butter to the pan. Transfer the meat to a roasting tin and pour over the juices from the frying pan. Add the shallots to the frying pan and cook for 3–4 minutes until soft.

3 Add the cherries and vinegar to the pan and cook for a minute, then add the wine and cook for 15 minutes, until the cherries are soft and the sauce reduced.

4 Roast the venison in the oven for up to 6–10 minutes, depending on how pink you like your meat. Remove from the oven, cover with foil and leave to rest for 5 minutes. Carve the venison and serve on warmed plates with the sauce spooned over. Serve with mashed sweet potato and green beans.

Serves 4

800g/1³⁄₄lb venison loin

15ml/1 tbsp olive oil

15g/¹⁄₂oz/1 tbsp butter

2 shallots, finely chopped

350g/12oz fresh black cherries, pitted

15ml/1 tbsp red wine vinegar

150ml/¹⁄₄ pint/²⁄₃ cup fruity red wine

salt and ground black pepper

mashed sweet potato and green beans, to serve

Energy 313kcal/1320kJ; Protein 45g; Carbohydrate 11g, of which sugars 11g; Fat 11g, of which saturates 4g; Cholesterol 108mg; Calcium 24mg; Fibre 1g; Sodium 134mg.

Partridge escabeche
Escabeche de perdiz

Serves 4–6

4 partridges, quartered

250ml/8fl oz/1 cup olive oil

250ml/8fl oz/1 cup white wine

2 onions, sliced

2 carrots, sliced

4 garlic cloves, peeled

1 bay leaf

5ml/1 tsp black peppercorns

5ml/1 tsp juniper berries

a few sprigs of fresh thyme

salt and ground black pepper

bread and a green salad, to serve.

Game dishes are a speciality of the Patagonian Andes, where wild partridges are plentiful, and hunting ranches thrive. Naturally lean, the meat is kept moist by gentle cooking in white wine, while the cloves and juniper berries add a wonderful flavour.

1 Season the partridge quarters with salt and pepper. Heat 45ml/3 tbsp of the oil in a large heavy frying pan and brown the partridge pieces for a few minutes on each side. Transfer to a large pan.

2 Add the vinegar, remaining oil, wine, vegetables, spices and herbs to the pan. Bring to the boil, cover and simmer for 30–35 minutes or until the partridge is tender. Remove the pan from the heat and set aside.

3 Leave the partridge to cool in the cooking liquid until completely cold. Then chill, preferably for 24 hours.

4 To serve, transfer the partridge to a serving plate and strain the liquid, discarding the vegetables and herbs and spices. Serve the partridge, with bread, a green salad, and a little of the strained liquid. Or, when cool, transfer the partridge and the liquid into large jars, and store in the refrigerator for up to 4 days.

Energy 431kcal/1802kJ; Protein 57g; Carbohydrate 0g, of which sugars 0g; Fat 22g, of which saturates 4g; Cholesterol 105mg; Calcium 73mg; Fibre 0g; Sodium 156mg.

Desserts
and Cakes

Argentina's sweet tooth is probably best typified by dulce de leche. This is loved all over South America but Argentinians have managed to work it into just about every sweet treat imaginable.

Milky rice puddings and sweet treats

To say that dulce de leche is a favourite among Argentinians would be a huge understatement. It is eaten at almost every meal of the day and for snacks in between. One of the best loved ways to serve it is with alfajores, two shortbread cookies sandwiched together with dulce de leche in the middle and then either rolled in coconut or dipped in chocolate.

Other sweet treats are often bought from patisseries, bakeries and ice cream parlours; many of the latter even offer home delivery, and busy hostesses will often order in desserts after spending all their time and energy on first and second courses. Family meals, however, are often finished with a home-baked tart, cookies or cake, or a creamy rice pudding.

Due to its Welsh influences Patagonia carries on a tradition of afternoon tea, and the famous fruit cake torta negra, or torta galesa, is served in tea houses in the region. Other home baking includes fritters and churros, inevitably served with dulce de leche, and often eaten for weekend breakfasts.

Grape jelly is uniquely Argentinian, typical of the Cuyo region where grapevines have been cultivated since the colonial era. It is served with creamy cheeses as a dessert or even appetizer.

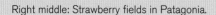
Right middle: Strawberry fields in Patagonia.

Rainy day fritters
Tortas fritas

The words tortas fritas translate as 'fried cakes' and the custom of eating these on rainy days with yerba mate tea can be traced back to the gauchos, who when camping out in la pampa would collect rainwater to make the mixture.

Makes 12

500g/1¼lb/4½ cups strong white flour

15ml/1 tbsp salt

30ml/2 tbsp caster (superfine) sugar

75g/3oz/6 tbsp lard or white cooking fat, diced

15g/½oz fresh yeast

150ml/¼ pint/⅔ cup tepid water

2 eggs, lightly beaten

lard, or vegetable oil for frying

caster (superfine) sugar, for dusting

1 Sift the flour, salt and sugar into a bowl. Add the lard and rub in with your fingertips until the mixture resembles fine breadcrumbs.

2 Blend the yeast and water together and add to the mixture with the eggs. Stir everything together to make a dough. Alternatively, put the flour, salt, sugar, lard and eggs in a food processor, and blend until combined, then add the yeast mixture and blend again until mixed.

3 Put the dough on a lightly floured surface, cover with clear film (plastic wrap) and leave in a warm place to rise for 30 minutes.

4 Reserve a small piece of dough for testing the fat temperature, then divide the rest into 12. Shape into rounds 3mm/⅛in thick. Make a small hole in the middle with your finger.

5 Melt enough lard, or oil, in a frying pan to a depth of about 2.5cm/1in. Heat until the fat sizzles when the small piece of dough is added.

6 Fry the fritters in batches of three or four until golden brown, turning once. Remove from the fat with a metal slotted spoon and drain on kitchen paper. Dust generously with caster sugar and serve hot.

Energy 267kcal/1120kJ; Protein 5g; Carbohydrate 35g, of which sugars 3g; Fat 13g, of which saturates 3g; Cholesterol 45mg; Calcium 64mg; Fibre 2g; Sodium 507mg.

Sweet fritters
Buñuelos

The Argentinian equivalent of doughnuts, these are usually eaten as a morning break or mid-afternoon snack, often accompanied by a cup of steaming mate. They can be filled with dulce de leche or apple purée as suggested here, or with créme pâtisserie.

1 Pour the oil into a heavy pan or deep-fat frying (it should come no more than half-way up the pan) and heat to 180°C/350°F.

2 While the oil is heating, sift the flour, baking powder and salt into a large bowl. Stir in the caster sugar and lemon rind. Make a hollow in the middle of the dry ingredients.

3 Beat the eggs and vanilla together in a small bowl with a fork, add to the hollow and mix together to make a thick sticky batter.

4 Using two spoons, drop balls of the dough into the hot oil, adding no more than three or four at a time. Fry for 2–3 minutes until puffed up, dark golden and crisp, turning in the oil, so that they brown evenly. Remove from the oil with a metal slotted spoon and drain. Continue to fry the fritters until all the batter is used up.

5 When the fritters are cool enough to handle, pipe the filling into the middle of each fritter, using a piping bag fitted with a small plain nozzle. Dust with icing sugar before serving.

Serves 4

175g/6oz/1½ cups plain (all-purpose) flour

30ml/2 tbsp baking powder

pinch of salt

45ml/3 tbsp caster (superfine) sugar

finely grated rind of 1 lemon

2 eggs

5ml/1 tsp vanilla extract

about 750ml/1¼ pints/ 3 cups vegetable oil, for deep-frying

dulce de leche, or apple purée, for filling

icing (confectioner's) sugar, for dusting

Energy 339kcal/1427kJ; Protein 8g; Carbohydrate 49g, of which sugars 12g; Fat 14g, of which saturates 2g; Cholesterol 119mg; Calcium 164mg; Fibre 2g; Sodium 930mg.

Chocolate-dipped churros
Churros con chocolate

Originally from Spain where they are usually served simply rolled in sugar, Argentinians have gone a step further and either serve churros filled with dulce de leche or dipped in chocolate. They are especially popular at seaside resorts.

1 Sift the flour on to a small sheet of baking parchment. Bring the water and salt to the boil in a pan. Tip in the flour and beat vigorously with a wooden spoon until the mixture is smooth. Remove the pan from the heat and let the dough cool a little. Spoon the mixture into a piping bag fitted with a large fluted nozzle.

2 Heat the oil in a deep-fat fryer or heavy pan to 180°C/350°C. Squeeze the piping bag over the pan, snipping off the lengths with scissors. Fry, in batches of four or six, until golden.

3 Remove with a slotted spoon and drain on kitchen paper. Sprinkle one end of each churros generously with sugar.

4 Break the chocolate into pieces and place in a heatproof bowl over a pan of near-boiling water. Leave until melted then stir gently. Holding the sugared end of each churros, dip the plain end into the chocolate. Lift out and let the excess drip back into the bowl, then place on a tray lined with baking parchment. Leave to set before serving.

Serves 4–6

500g/1¼lb/4½ cups strong white flour

5ml/1 tsp salt

500ml/17fl oz/generous 2 cups water

115g/4oz plain (semi-sweet) chocolate

vegetable oil, for deep-frying

caster (superfine) sugar, for sprinkling

Energy 478kcal/2016kJ; Protein 9g; Carbohydrate 79g, of which sugars 15g; Fat 16g, of which saturates 5g; Cholesterol 1mg; Calcium 123mg; Fibre 3g; Sodium 331mg.

Toffee sauce
Dulce de leche

Makes 400ml/2 cups

1 litre/1³/₄ pints/4 cups whole milk

350g/12oz/1³/₄ cups caster (superfine) sugar

150g/5oz glucose

5ml/1 tsp vanilla extract

1.5ml/¹/₄ tsp bicarbonate of soda (baking soda)

Cook's tip If the sauce begins to stick and burn at the bottom of the pan before it is ready, quickly pour it into a clean pan, lower the heat a little and continue cooking and stirring.

Dulce de leche is a sticky sweet caramelized sugar and milk mixture, widely used as a filling, frosting or topping in desserts, pastries, cakes and cookies. It can be bought ready-made in cans and jars, or you can prepare your own – a bit time-consuming, but very worthwhile and much more economical.

1 Put the milk and sugar into a heavy pan on a very low heat. Add the glucose and vanilla and heat, stirring until the sugar dissolves. Continue cooking for 30–45 minutes, stirring frequently with a wooden spoon.

2 Blend the bicarbonate of soda with 15ml/ 1 tbsp cold water and stir into the mixture. Turn up the heat a little and cook for 20–30 minutes or until it reaches 107°C/225°F on a sugar thermometer, stirring constantly towards the end of cooking to prevent it sticking.

3 When ready, the mixture should be thick and a rich tan colour. To test, lift your spoon and drizzle some of the sauce over the surface, if it forms a ribbon that does not disappear after 10 seconds, it is ready. Straight away, plunge the base of the pan into a sink containing some cold water, to cool.

4 Leave the mixture to cool completely, stirring occasionally, then transfer to a bowl, or a large jar with a lide, cover and chill in the refrigerator until ready to use.

Energy 1137kcal/4773kJ; Protein 33g; Carbohydrate 173g, of which sugars 106g; Fat 39g, of which saturates 25g; Cholesterol 135mg; Calcium 1192mg; Fibre 0g; Sodium 929mg.

Grape preserve
Arrope

Serves 4–6

500g/1¼lb red grapes

375g/13oz caster (superfine) sugar

Arrope originated in Spain where it is made from freshly pressed grape juice. Introduced to Argentina during colonization, it is sometimes made with cactus fruit instead of grapes. Serve spooned over fresh figs, with shortbread biscuits.

1 Wash the grapes and place in wide shallow bowl or container. Sprinkle the sugar over the grapes, cover and chill overnight.

2 The following day, tip the grapes and sugary syrup into a pan and cook over a low heat, stirring frequently until the sugar dissolves. Continue cooking for 45 minutes to 1 hour or until the liquid turns a deep dark syrupy colour, stirring occasionally.

3 Strain the liquid through a fine sieve into hot sterilized jars and seal.

4 Leave to cool, then store in the refrigerator, where it will keep for up to two weeks. Serve with fresh figs, accompanied by shortbread.

Cook's Tip As well as being served as a dessert, arrope can be spread on bread, or spooned over goat's cheese.

Energy 296kcal/1264kJ; Protein 0g; Carbohydrate 78g, of which sugars 78g; Fat 0g, of which saturates 0g; Cholesterol 0mg; Calcium 17mg; Fibre 0g; Sodium 5mg.

Fig conserve
Dulce de higos

Figs grow in abundance in Argentina, but their season is short, so as well as eating them fresh they are dried for enjoying at Christmas, bottled in syrup or made into jams and conserves; a good way to use slightly under-ripe fruit.

1 Carefully wash the figs and pat dry on kitchen paper. Trim off the top stalk ends with a sharp knife, then either gently pull the figs in half by hand, or cut with the knife.

2 Place cutside up in a single layer in a shallow dish and thickly sprinkle over the sugar. Cover with plastic wrap and leave in the refrigerator for at least 8 hours or overnight.

3 Transfer the figs, sugar and juices into a heavy pan and add the clove.

4 Heat gently until the sugar has all dissolved, stirring occasionally. Add the lemon rind to the pan with the whisky or rum, if using.

5 Bring to the boil and simmer for 30 minutes, stirring occasionally, until all the juices have evaporated and the mixture is very thick.

6 Remove the clove, then spoon the conserve into hot sterilized jars and seal. Leave to cool, then store in the refrigerator. Once opened, use within six weeks.

Makes about 500g/1¼lb

500g/1¼lb firm ripe figs

375g/13oz/scant 2 cups caster (superfine) sugar

1 whole clove

finely grated rind of 1 lemon

30ml/2 tbsp whisky or rum (optional)

Energy 1693kcal/7225kJ; Protein 7g; Carbohydrate 441g, of which sugars 441g; Fat 2g, of which saturates 1g; Cholesterol 0mg; Calcium 228mg; Fibre 12g; Sodium 34mg.

Caramel-filled cookies
Alfajores

Pairs of light golden biscuits filled with dulce de leche are one of the most popular sweets in Argentina, especially on the coast where you can buy them at any beach kiosk. It is estimated around six million of these are consumed daily! There are many variations; some are simply dusted with sugar, others coated in chocolate; some – as here – rolled in coconut.

1 Beat the butter, sugar and lemon rind in a large bowl until light and fluffy. Beat in the egg yolks, one by one, and the vanilla extract.

2 Sift the flour, baking powder and bicarbonate of soda over the mixture, add the semolina and mix together to make a smooth dough, taking care not to over-handle it. Wrap in clear film (plastic wrap) and chill in the refrigerator for at least 30 minutes.

3 Preheat the oven to 180°C/350°F/Gas 4, and line two large baking sheets with baking parchment.

4 Roll out the dough on a lightly floured surface until 5mm/¼in thick. Cut into circles with a 4cm/1½in cookie cutter and carefully transfer to the baking sheets, spacing slightly apart.

5 Bake for about 8 minutes or until set, but not browned. Remove from the oven, leave on the sheets for a few minutes, then transfer to a wire rack to cool completely.

6 Spread the underside of a cooled cookie with a heaped teaspoon of dulce de leche, then sandwich together with another cookie, gently pressing together, until the dulce de leche just oozes a little out of the sides.

7 Place the coconut on a plate and roll the edges of the cookie sandwich over the coconut, so that it sticks to the dulce de leche. Repeat with the remaining cookies.

Makes 12

100g/3¾oz/scant ½ cup butter, softened

75g/3oz/scant ½ cup caster (superfine) sugar

finely grated zest of 1 lemon

2 egg yolks

5ml/1 tsp vanilla extract

100g/3¾oz/scant 1 cup plain (all-purpose) flour

5ml/1 tsp baking powder

5ml/1 tsp bicarbonate of soda (baking soda)

150g/5oz/scant 1 cup semolina

dulce de leche, for filling

desiccated (dry unsweetened) coconut, to coat

Energy 219kcal/919kJ; Protein 4g; Carbohydrate 31g, of which sugars 11g; Fat 10g, of which saturates 6g; Cholesterol 57mg; Calcium 88mg; Fibre 1g; Sodium 381mg.

Quince tart
Pastafrola de membrillo

Pastafrola, like many classic Argentinian recipes, is Italian in origin. In Italy this shortbread-like pastry features in a range of desserts and bakes, but in Argentina it is only used to make this delicious tart filled with quince preserve or sometimes with sweet-potato jam.

Serves 6–8

200g/7oz/1 cup caster (superfine) sugar

200g/7oz/scant 1 cup butter, softened

1 egg

1 egg yolk

5ml/1 tsp vanilla extract

400g/14oz/3½ cups self-raising (self-rising) flour

400g/14oz/1¾ cups quince jelly (membrillo), cut into small cubes, or the same quantity of apple purée or dulce de leche

Cook's Tip Quince jelly, or the Spanish equivalent membrillo, is often eaten with cheese, and can be found in the cheese section of a supermarket, rather than the jams and preserves section.

1 Put the sugar and butter in a large bowl and beat together with a wooden spoon until smooth and creamy. Beat the egg, yolk and vanilla together. Add to the creamed mixture a little at a time, beating well between each addition and adding a teaspoonful of the flour if it starts to curdle.

2 Sift the flour over the mixture and gently mix in to make a dough. Lightly knead on a floured surface for a few seconds until smooth, then cut off one-third of the pastry.

3 Wrap the pastry separately in clear film (plastic wrap) and chill for 30 minutes.

4 Put a baking sheet in the oven and preheat to 160°C/325°F/Gas 3. Put the quince jelly in a pan and add 45ml/3 tbsp water. Heat gently, breaking up the jelly with a fork until melted and smooth. Leave to cool a little.

5 Take the larger piece of pastry out of the refrigerator, roll out on a floured surface and use to line a 23–25cm/9–10 in loose-based flan tin (quiche pan), 3cm/1¼in deep. Press the pastry into the sides and trim the edge. Pour the quince jelly over the base of the pastry case and shake gently to distribute evenly.

6 Roll out the small piece of pastry into a rectangle the same length as the flan tin. Cut into strips slightly smaller than 2cm/¾in wide with a sharp knife and arrange in a lattice pattern over the jelly filling.

7 Bake the tart for about 40 minutes, or until the lattice is golden brown. Leave to cool in the tin before cutting and serving.

Energy 620kcal/2615kJ; Protein 6g; Carbohydrate 104g, of which sugars 67g; Fat 23g, of which saturates 14g; Cholesterol 108mg; Calcium 194mg; Fibre 3g; Sodium 351mg.

Ice cream with whisky
Don Pedro

Argentinians love ice cream, and are justly proud of the high-quality Italian style 'helados' that are available. Don Pedro is a popular dessert in many restaurants, made with good-quality vanilla and a generous amount of whisky. Ice cream and whisky are also blended together as a cocktail, decorated with grated chocolate.

1 Chill four ice cream glasses or individual dishes in the refrigerator or freezer (make sure the glasses are suitable for freezing if you take this option) until well-chilled.

2 Spoon 15ml/1 tbsp dulce de leche into each glass, then add two scoops of ice cream. Add 30ml/2 tbsp of whisky each.

3 Sprinkle half the hazelnuts, cherries, grated chocolate and crushed amaretti biscuits over the top, then add a final scoop of ice cream.

4 Drizzle 15ml/1 tbsp chocolate sauce over the top. Finish with the remaining hazelnuts, cherries, grated chocolate and amaretti biscuits and a wafer. Eat immediately.

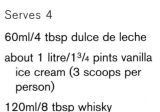

Serves 4

60ml/4 tbsp dulce de leche

about 1 litre/1³/₄ pints vanilla ice cream (3 scoops per person)

120ml/8 tbsp whisky

50g/2oz/¹/₂ cup toasted chopped hazelnuts

16 preserved black cherries

50g/2oz dark (bittersweet) chocolate, grated

12 amaretti biscuits, roughly crushed

60ml/4 tbsp chocolate sauce

4 ice cream wafers

Energy 593kcal/2482kJ; Protein 9g; Carbohydrate 62g, of which sugars 57g; Fat 29g, of which saturates 12g; Cholesterol 39mg; Calcium 211mg; Fibre 2g; Sodium 116mg.

Rice pudding
Arroz con leche

Rice pudding is a popular dessert in many countries. In Argentina, it is usually made on the hob, rather than oven-baked, so has a thick creamy consistency. This version is enriched not only with with egg yolks, cream and butter, but also with the Italian cheese, mascarpone, so is extremely rich, and utterly delicious.

1 Soak the rice in cold water for 20 minutes. Put the milk, sugar and vanilla pods in a heavy pan and bring to the boil. Drain the rice and add to the milk.

2 Bring back to the boil, lower the heat and gently simmer, uncovered, for 30 minutes, or until the rice is tender and has absorbed most of the milk. Stir occasionally, especially towards the end of cooking to prevent it sticking.

3 Remove the pan from the heat and stir in the butter, mascarpone and cream, followed by the egg yolks.

4 Spoon the rice pudding into warmed bowls and serve hot, if you wish. Or allow to cool, then chill in the refrigerator before serving cold. Drizzle a little honey over the top and scatter with sultanas, candied citrus peel, preserved black cherries and sprigs of fresh mint.

Serves 4–6

200g/7oz/1 cup pudding rice

1.2 litres/2 pints/5 cups whole milk

115g/4oz/generous ½ cup sugar

1 vanilla pod, split in half

50g/2oz/4 tbsp butter, softened

115g/4oz/½ cup mascarpone

100ml/3½fl oz/scant ½ cup double (heavy) cream

2 egg yolks

15ml/1 tbsp clear honey

sultanas (golden raisins), chopped candied citrus peel, chopped preserved black cherries, and sprigs of fresh mint, to decorate

Energy 578kcal/2405kJ; Protein 11g; Carbohydrate 57g, of which sugars 32g; Fat 34g, of which saturates 21g; Cholesterol 154mg; Calcium 280mg; Fibre 0g; Sodium 241mg.

Creamy corn pudding
Mazamorra

This dish was created during colonial times in north-western Argentina, where corn is still the main staple grain. Similar to rice pudding, it is often served to celebrate holidays such as National Flag Day on 20th June.

1 Put the corn in a pan and pour over the water. Leave to soak for at least 2 hours. Bring the corn to the boil, then lower the heat and simmer for 45 minutes until the corn is tender.

2 Drain well, then tip the corn back into the pan and mash well with a potato masher or a fork. Transfer the corn to a bowl. Pour the milk into the pan (there's no need to rinse it first).

3 Add the sugar and vanilla pods to the milk and heat slowly, stirring occasionally until the sugar dissolves. Bring to the boil, then add the mashed corn and cook for 15 minutes stirring occasionally with a wooden spoon.

4 Spoon into bowls and serve warm, or at room temperature, with a sprinkling of cinnamon and drizzled with honey or arrope.

Serves 4–6

500g/1¼lb/2¾ cups dried white corn kernels

2 litres/3½ pints/8 cups water

1 litre/1¾ pints/4 cups whole milk

200g/7oz/1 cup sugar

2 vanilla pods, split lengthways

5ml/1 tsp ground cinnamon, to sprinkle

honey, to serve

Energy 319kcal/1347kJ; Protein 8g; Carbohydrate 57g, of which sugars 8g; Fat 44g, of which saturates 4g; Cholesterol 23mg; Calcium 203mg; Fibre 3g; Sodium 74mg.

Custard pots
Ambrosia

Serves 4

200g/7oz/1 cup caster (superfine) sugar

200ml/7fl oz/scant 1 cup water

1 egg

3 egg yolks

250ml/8fl oz/1 cup whole milk

finely grated rind of 1 lemon

shortbread biscuits, to serve

Whisking hot sugar syrup into the egg and milk mixture gives these custards a wonderfully smooth creamy texture. They are simply flavoured with lemon and make a delicious dessert served with shortbread biscuits.

1 Put the sugar and water in a heavy pan and heat gently until the sugar has dissolved.

2 Increase the heat and boil the sugar solution rapidly until it reaches 107°C/225°F on a sugar thermometer, or when a few drops added to a cup of cold water form a fine thread.

3 Meanwhile, whisk the egg, egg yolks, milk and lemon rind together in a jug (pitcher).

4 When the sugar syrup is ready, turn down the heat as low as possible and pour in the egg and milk mixture, whisking all the time. Cook, stirring constantly, until the mixture has just thickened. Don't overcook or it may curdle.

5 Allow the custard to cool a little, then pour into small dishes or glasses. Leave to cool, then chill for several hours until lightly set. Serve with shortbread biscuits.

Energy 306kcal/1291kJ; Protein 6g; Carbohydrate 55g, of which sugars 55g; Fat 8g, of which saturates 3g; Cholesterol 219mg; Calcium 105mg; Fibre 0g; Sodium 57mg.

Christmas cake
Pan dulce

Rich and buttery, full of the warm scent of vanilla, and packed with dried fruit and nuts, this is a cross between a sweet bread and a light-textured cake. Italian in origin, where it is known as panettone, in Argentina it is traditionally served after Christmas dinner.

Makes a 1kg/2¼lb loaf

For the starter dough

7g/½oz fresh yeast

20ml/4 tsp warm water

175g/6oz/1½ cups strong bread flour

1 large egg, lightly beaten

For the pan dulce dough

175g/6oz/1½ cups strong bread flour

115g/4oz/scant 1 cup caster (superfine) sugar

pinch of salt

7g/½oz fresh yeast

120ml/4fl oz/½ cup milk

10ml/2 tsp vanilla extract

5ml/1 tsp orange blossom water or orange liqueur

finely grated rind of ½ orange

finely grated rind of ½ lemon

85g/3½oz/7 tbsp unsalted (sweet) butter, softened

250g/9oz/1½ cups dried and chopped candied fruits (orange and lemon peel, raisins, apricots, cranberries, citrus peel)

250g/9oz/1½ cups mixed nuts (walnuts, hazelnuts, almonds, pecans), lightly toasted and roughly chopped

beaten egg, to glaze

glacé icing and candied fruit, to decorate

1 For the starter dough, blend the yeast with the water in a small bowl. Put the flour in a bowl and make a hollow in the middle. Add the yeast mixture and egg to the hollow and mix to a smooth dough. Cover the bowl with clear film (plastic wrap) and leave at room temperature for about 45 minutes until doubled in size.

2 When the starter dough has risen, make the pan dulce dough. Put the flour in a bowl and stir in the sugar and salt. Make a hollow in the middle. Blend the yeast with the milk. Add to the hollow with the vanilla, orange blossom water and citrus rind. Mix to an elastic dough; it should be quite soft.

3 Turn out the dough onto a lightly floured surface and work in the butter. Return the dough to the bowl, cover with plastic wrap, and set aside in a warm place to rise for 2–4 hours or until doubled in volume.

4 Line a 15cm/6in deep cake tin (pan) with a double layer of baking parchment, extending it 12cm/5in above the rim. Turn out the dough and work in the fruit and nuts. Place in the tin, cover and leave to rise until the dough is 2.5cm/1in above the top of the tin. Preheat the oven to 160°C/325°F/Gas 3.

5 When risen, brush the top of the loaf with beaten egg and cut a cross on the top with a sharp knife. Bake for 45–55 minutes or until well risen and dark golden. Leave in the tin for 10 minutes, then transfer to a wire rack to cool. Decorate with glacé icing and candied fruits.

Cook's Tips Egg and butter-enriched doughs take a long time to rise, so start early. Don't put the dough in a very warm place to speed up rising as the butter will melt and make the dough greasy. Make two 500g/1¼lb pan dolce if you prefer; bake for 35–40 minutes.

Energy 4845kcal/20,284kJ; Protein 91g; Carbohydrate 566g, of which sugars 297g; Fat 263g, of which saturates 64g; Cholesterol 688mg; Calcium 1181mg; Fibre 30g; Sodium 1100mg.

Black Welsh cake
Torta Negra

A group of settlers from Wales came to the Chubut river region in Patagonia in the late 18th century. The area retains many Welsh traditions such as 'afternoon tea' and this cake is served in quaint tea houses. It is traditional to have a black Welsh cake as the bottom tier of a wedding cake.

1 Put the sugar, honey, raisins and water in a pan and slowly bring to the boil. Cover and simmer over a low heat for 5 minutes.

2 Cut the butter into chunks, add to the pan, re-cover and let it stand for about 5 minutes until the butter has melted and the mixture cooled a little.

3 Preheat the oven to 150°C/300°F/Gas 2. Line the base of a deep 20cm/8in round cake tin (pan) with baking parchment.

4 Tip the warm raisin mixture into a large bowl. Sift over the flour, bicarbonate of soda and cinnamon and use a wooden spoon to gently mix and fold together until almost combined. Add the nuts, fruit and brandy and fold into the mixture until well mixed.

5 Spoon and scrape the mixture into the tin and level the top with the back of a spoon. Make a very slight dip in the middle, so that the cake rises evenly.

6 Place the cake in the oven and bake for 1 hour, or until a skewer inserted into the middle of the cake comes out clean.

7 Leave to cool in the tin for 15 minutes, then turn out onto a wire rack and leave to cool completely before slicing and serving with tea.

Makes 8–12 slices

- 200g/7oz/scant cup soft dark brown sugar
- 30ml/2 tbsp clear honey
- 200g/7oz/generous cup raisins
- 250ml/8fl oz/1 cup water
- 225g/8oz/1 cup butter
- 300g/11oz/2³⁄₄ cups plain (all-purpose) flour
- 10ml/2 tsp bicarbonate of soda (baking soda)
- 5ml/1 tsp ground cinnamon
- 75g/3oz/³⁄₄ cup walnut halves
- 50g/2oz/¹⁄₂ cup blanched almonds
- 100g/3¹⁄₂ oz/¹⁄₂ cup candied fruit, roughly chopped
- 100g/3¹⁄₂oz/generous ¹⁄₂ cup prunes, roughly chopped
- 100ml/7 tbsp brandy

Energy 437kcal/1833kJ; Protein 5g; Carbohydrate 58g, of which sugars 39g; Fat 23g, of which saturates 10g; Cholesterol 40mg; Calcium 88mg; Fibre 4g; Sodium 338mg.

Bread pudding
Budin de pan

Serves 6

- 100g/3³/₄oz/scant 1 cup caster (superfine) sugar
- 200ml/7fl oz/scant 1 cup whole milk
- 75g/3oz/³/₄ cup caster sugar
- 200g/7oz white bread, at least one-day old, crusts removed, processed to coarse crumbs
- 50ml/2fl oz/¹/₄ cup double (heavy) cream
- 5ml/1 tsp vanilla extract
- 2 eggs, lightly beaten
- finely grated rind of 1 lemon
- finely grated rind of 1 orange
- a handful of raisins
- a handful of chopped walnuts
- whipped cream and dulce de leche to serve

Every culture seems to have a bread pudding recipe, originally a thrify way to use up leftover stale bread. The Argentinian version is now a glorious dessert in its own right, flavoured with sweet caramel and tangy citrus rind, and enriched with cream.

1 To make the caramel, put the sugar in a heavy pan and heat gently, without stirring, until it is dissolved. Increase the heat and boil rapidly for a few minutes until the syrup turns to a rich golden brown.

2 Pour into a non-stick loaf tin (pan), measuring about 25 x 12 x 6cm/10 x 4¹/₂ x 2¹/₂in, and tilt to partly coat the sides of the tin.

3 Preheat the oven to 180°C/350°F/Gas 4. Pour the milk into the pan used to make caramel. Add the sugar and heat until warm, stirring occasionally to dissolve the sugar.

4 Remove the pan from the heat and stir in the breadcrumbs, cream, vanilla, and beaten eggs. Mix the lemon and orange rind, raisins and walnuts in a bowl. Pour over the bread and milk mixture and stir together. Pour and scrape into the caramel-coated tin.

5 Put the tin in a deep roasting pan and pour in enough hot water to come 5–7.5cm/2–3in up the sides of the tin. Bake for 1 hour or until lightly set. Remove the loaf tin from the hot water and leave to cool. Chill for 8 hours, at least, or overnight. Turn out of the tin and slice. Serve with whipped cream and dulce de leche.

Energy 548kcal/2296kJ; Protein 14g; Carbohydrate 68g, of which sugars 53g; Fat 26g, of which saturates 11g; Cholesterol 124mg; Calcium 313mg; Fibre 3g; Sodium 303mg.

Index